INSANITY!

INSANITY!

How can Sanity and Civility Be Restored to a Culture in the Process of Being Turned Over to Itself?

Kerry D. McRoberts

RESOURCE *Publications* • Eugene, Oregon

INSANITY!
How can Sanity and Civility Be Restored to a Culture in the Process of Being Turned Over to Itself?

Copyright © 2018 Kerry D. McRoberts. All rights reserved. Except for brief quotations in critical publications or reviews, no part of this book may be reproduced in any manner without prior written permission from the publisher. Write: Permissions, Wipf and Stock Publishers, 199 W. 8th Ave., Suite 3, Eugene, OR 97401.

Resource Publications
An Imprint of Wipf and Stock Publishers
199 W. 8th Ave., Suite 3
Eugene, OR 97401

www.wipfandstock.com

PAPERBACK ISBN: 978-1-5326-4971-4
HARDCOVER ISBN: 978-1-5326-4972-1
EBOOK ISBN: 978-1-5326-4973-8

Manufactured in the U.S.A.

All Scripture quotations, unless otherwise indicated, are taken from the HOLY BIBLE: NEW INTERNATION VERSION®; NIV®. Copyright ©1973, 1978, 1984 by International Bible Society. Used by permission of Zondervan Publishing House. All rights reserved.

For,
Ryan, Jamie, Daphne, Hayley, Payton, Sydney & Wesley

Contents

Acknowledgements | ix
Glossary of Terms | xi
Introduction—'Freedom Without Posters | xix

Chapter 1: INSANITY! | 1
Chapter 2: 'A Unique Understanding of the Time of the End' | 9
Chapter 3: The Sermon on the Mount: Mt. 5:1–7:29 | 21
Chapter 4: 'Do Not Commit Adultery': Mt. 5:27-30 | 32
Chapter 5: Marriage and Divorce: Mt. 5:31-32 | 39
Chapter 6: Oaths: Mt. 5:32-37 | 53
Chapter 7: 'An Eye for an Eye'—Revenge: Mt. 5:38-42 | 63
Chapter 8: 'Love Your Enemies': Mt. 5:43-48 | 68
Chapter 9: 'When You Give': Mt. 6:1-4 | 75
Chapter 10: 'When You Pray': Mt. 6:5-14 | 81
Chapter 11: 'When You Fast': Mt. 6:16-18 | 86
Chapter 12: 'Treasures in Heaven': Mt. 6:19-21 | 90
Chapter 13: 'Do Not Worry': Mt. 6:25-34 | 94
Chapter 14: Judging Others: Mt. 7:1, 3, 12 | 98
Chapter 15: 'Enter Through the Narrow Gate': Mt. 13-14; 21-23 | 108
Chapter 16: A Wise Builder: Mt. 7:24 | 114

Appendix 1: America's Christian Heritage | 123
Bibliography | 129

Acknowledgements

IN THIS BOOK, I speak of the Sermon on the Mount taking narrative form in the lives of believers; that is, people who live (or lived) in the reality of their future resurrection and consequently, they give profound meaning to the lives of countless others, to include myself.

They are too many for me to mention here, but among them are: J.I. Packer, Walter R. Martin, Harold Lindsell, Ronald Enroth, Leonard Sweet, Glen Menzies, Phil Mayo, Allen Tennison, Warren Bullock, Amy Anderson, Frank Cole, Dale Carpenter—And their sons are not far behind them, Dave and Cal—Rick Ross, Don Detrick, Don Ross, Jim Heugel, Darrell Hobson, David Grant, Dan Womack, Dave Frederick, Phil Fernandez, Virgil Brown, and Jim Schultz. Julie Snyder, an extraordinary educator, edited my work; and Dustin Hirschy and Kimberly Jones also daily incarnate Jesus' sermon. And most of all, Vicki's life is beautifully framed in the Beatitudes, and as well, my daughters, Kari Schultz and Traci Brakefield.

I have pastored four churches and lectured in four schools. To each of the congregations and student bodies, a special dedication of this book is extended: Bethel (New Harvest) Assembly of God; Sumner Assembly of God, Kings Circle Assembly of God and Bayside Community Church. And Northwest University, Trinity Bible College, North Central University and the Assemblies of God Theological Seminary.

And finally, this book is dedicated to seven most wonderful people who I love and pray the Sermon on the Mount will take narrative form in their lives as they enjoy living—throughout their lives—in the greatest nation on the face of the earth: Ryan, Jamie, Daphne, Hayley, Payton, Sydney and Wesley.

Glossary of Terms

American exceptionalism: *Refers to U.S. America's unique or exceptional form of republic democratic government. The Constitution and Declaration of Independence presuppose that sustainable freedom requires religion (acknowledgement of God and His created order), and morality.*

Autonomy: *Literally, self-law; the autonomous person is their own law; they are a law unto themselves.*

Bohemian man: *In this book, used as a description of hippies in the 60s; an artist, poet, etc., who lives in an unconventional, nonconformist way.*

Boomers: *Re: Barna Trends, 2017—The Boomer generation were born 1946–1964.*

Church; The: *[Protestant] Evangelicals have no official spokesperson or centralized church. Evangelicals speak for themselves; but we are united in the historic Christian faith "once delivered"—especially, "Salvation is through faith alone, by grace alone in Christ alone;" and the sacred creeds of the church, e.g., Apostles Creed, Nicene Creed, Chalcedon, etc.).*

Covenant: *A Biblical covenant is a mutually binding agreement between two parties who willingly promise to faithfully live by its terms. God has chosen to relate to his creation and all creatures; and specifically, Israel and the church, through covenant relationships (cf. Deut. 28-29; Lev. 26).*

Created Order (**Natural Order**): *The Biblical God is moral; and the created order, both the natural order and uniquely, humanity as God's image bearers, reflect his moral nature (Rom. 1:19-20).*

Cultural appropriation: *A charge made against people who have allegedly hijacked elements common to one culture and applied them to a different culture.*

Glossary of Terms

Culture: *The cultivated customs (norms), ideas (worldview), institutions (representative symbols, e.g., flag, bald eagle, Statue of Liberty, etc.), language, arts, etc., of a given people in a given period and civilization, the way of life of a particular people, esp. as shown in their ordinary behavior and habits, their attitudes toward each other, and their moral and religious beliefs.*

Descriptive definition: *A definition founded on observation. In the case of Christianity, for example, a definition of Christian faith founded on the observed behavioral of Christians.*

Elders: *Re: Barna Trends, 2017—The elder generation were born before 1946 (Also referred to as "builders").*

Evangelical/Born-Again Christian: *Re: Barna Trends, 2017, Evangelical, born-again Christians have a personal relationship with Christ; assurance of salvation; believe in the atoning death of Christ for human sin; faith is deeply important to their lives; feel responsible for the sharing of their faith; believe Satan exists; believe Jesus lived a sinless life on earth; believe in the full-authority of the Bible; believe salvation is by grace alone, through faith alone in Christ alone and God is all-knowing (omniscient), all-powerful (omnipotent) and omnipresent (present everywhere) and perfect deity—God is from everlasting to everlasting; he is sovereign over all his creation.*

Eschatology: *Eschatology is the study of human history's end. Used in this book as a unique understanding of the time of the End.*

Ethics: *Human ethics presuppose a personal transcendent. Ethics relate to "oughtness," that is, ethics inform us how human beings ought to behave. (Please see morals below for a distinction between ethics and morals).*

Exclusivism: *Founded on two premises: (1) The Holy Spirit's internal witness to saving faith in Christ is assurance of personal salvation and (2) apart from a person having the Spirit, they do not belong to Christ (Romans 8:9; John 14:6; Acts 4:12).*

Existentialism: *A philosophy about existence. Existentialism defines human nature by our moral motions, that is, the choices we make—"I am my choices" (Sartre). To be a "self-made" man or woman is to have created one's own nature through their choices. Whereas there is truth in existentialism, it is half-truth. In other words, we are free moral agents but our moral nature is related to our special creation in the image of a personal, living God. The choices we make say something about our character but not our origins, that* is, we are not creating our nature through our choices, we are rather expressing our nature.

Evil: *Following each day of creation, God proclaimed his creation, "good." Evil is not the opposite of good but rather, it is the spoiling or perversion of good. Therefore, evil does not exist apart from good; evil is a parasite on good—heresy does not exist apart from truth for it is the perversion of truth; hate does not exist apart from love and lust, greed and prejudice do not exist on their own but rather they are a perversion of purity, prosperity, and human dignity.*

Fact/value dichotomy: *Progressive historical skepticism is the mold for the forming of the "fact/value dichotomy." The fact/value dichotomy holds that we are not able to derive a value from a fact, or an 'ought' from an 'is.' In practical terms, "Since history cannot be relied upon to teach me anything about today, I need to interpret facts in light of contemporary social norms and values." Therefore, the separation of facts and their interpretation is "a given"—an unspoken assumption—in the thinking of the secular progressive.*

Fascism: *An intolerant authoritarian or totalitarian form of government—fascism is economically and socially oppressive; life is centered in the state's control; nothing is outside the state.*

Gen-Xers: *Re: Barna Trends, 2017—The Gen-Xer generation were born between 1965–1983.*

God's Image: *We are created in God's "likeness" and "image." The "likeness-image" of God refers to humanity's special connection with God; our special connection with God makes it possible for humanity to be a meaningful reflection of God—Kierkegaard concludes that the relationship between God and man is what makes man a man (The special relationship Kierkegaard refers to is founded on creation, not salvation by grace, through faith in Jesus Christ).*

Hedonism: *Pleasure is an end in-itself; therefore, the good is that which brings carnal pleasure and evil is the opposite, that is, evil is the absence of pleasure. (Please see the definition of evil above).*

Holy: *A synonym of sacred; meaning to set apart unto God.*

Homosexuality/Homoeroticism: *In this book, the distinction is between a person's orientation or inclination towards intimacy with a person of the same-sex (homosexuality) and active same-sex relations (homoeroticism).*

Glossary of Terms

Hyper-Modernism: *Unbridled human autonomy; absolutely no restrictions on human expression or moral motions.*

Human Dignity: *Human beings are created in God's image and therefore, a person's dignity is inviolable, that is, God confers upon all humans an elevated status—personal dignity, that must be honored and never degraded.*

Illumination: *Used in this book to refer to the Holy Spirit's aid in providing insight (understanding) and application of Scripture to a person's life.*

Individualism: *Self-interest is considered the proper goal of all human action.*

Intrinsic: *Belonging to the inherent or essential nature of a thing; not dependent on something else external to it.*

Kingdom of God/Kingdom of Heaven: *God's reign embodied in Jesus.*

Lawlessness: *Relative to contemporary culture, lawlessness does not necessarily say, "I know this is wrong but I'm going to do it anyway," rather lawlessness says, "Who's to say what right and wrong is?"*

LGBTQ: *Acronym for Lesbian-Gay-Bisexual-Transgender-Queer or Questioning. Formerly, the term "queer" was a pejorative used to degrade or demean a gay person. For many in the LGBTQ community, the term "queer" is still considered offensive. However, in recent years younger people in junior and senior high school and college/university campuses have reclaimed the term and use it as a "badge of honor." "Questioning" refers to someone who is unsure of their gender identity and therefore they are questioning their sexual orientation.*

Microaggression: *A term common on university campuses for a small action or choice of words that although on their face pose no malicious intent but subtly represent a kind of violence nonetheless.*

Millennials: *Re: Barna Trends, 2017—Millennials are people born between 1984–2002.*

Morals: *Morals relate to "is-ness," that is, morals describe what human behavior is. (Please see ethics above for a distinction between ethics and morals).*

Narcissism: *An excessive interest in one's own comfort, convenience, importance—the gap between "self" and others is extraordinarily wide. To some degree, all fallen human beings suffer from varying degrees of narcissism.*

Glossary of Terms

Nihilism: *There is nothing—That is, life is [absolutely] without meaning or purpose.*

Normative definition: *A "normative" understanding is the definition of another's position as founded on primary sources. For example, a normative understanding of Christian faith is an understanding founded on the New Testament.*

Penal recompense: *The "due penalty"—The unnatural sexual aberration (homosexuality) of women and men is itself punishment for the fact that they do not pay God the honor which is His due (cf. Romans 1:26-27).*

Pederasty: *Sexual relations between a man and a boy instead of mutual adult-adult homosexuality.*

Politically correct: *An amoral substitute for moral knowledge; political correctness is a self-regarding "ethic" that conforms divine law to progressive political ends.*

Politicizing Christian Faith: *Using the Bible/faith to express essentially political points that have lost touch with biblical truth.*

Post-church culture: *The marginalizing of the church; the church is in exile and therefore, it is removed from the public square. (Many born-again Christians no longer see the need of the formal or institutional church; although this does not mean that they do not see the need to gather together with other believers in private settings).*

Post-human: *"Post-human" is a complex, multi-layered discussion, used in this book it refers to redefining "human" as something other than an image-bearer of God.*

Practicing Christian: *Self-identified Christians who say their faith is very important in their lives and have attended a worship service within the past month (A George Barna category related to in this book).*

***Prima facie* evidence:** *Lit.: "On the face of it"—Evidence that is good and sufficient on its face.*

Progressive: *A secular progressive believes that their place in history is the ultimate, climatic point in human history—all that can be known, is now known. Progressive secularists are therefore historical skeptics—history, in the*

Glossary of Terms

thinking of the progressive, is incapable of providing substantive knowledge about the changing world.

Profane: *Lit. "outside the temple;" irreligious; not sacred—displays contempt or disrespect for holy or sacred things.*

Public Square: *A metaphor for all forums represented by citizens to come together to debate, deliberate and weigh the implications of their common life. The places and means for citizens to come together range from the United States Congress to the inter-net to coffee shops to op-ed columns to radio talk-shows to front porches and town squares.*

Relativism: *A theory of ethics that appeals to a relative basis of judgement as opposed to absolutes.*

Religious pluralism: *Religious pluralism's "inclusiveness" insists that all the world's religions are equal contexts for "salvation" or "liberation"—all humanity will ultimately partake of God's salvation.*

Sacred: *Used in this book to refer to the inherent value of human dignity.*

Sanctuary campuses: *College/University campuses that promise to protect undocumented students from deportation.*

Secularization: *The removal of the religious consensus from society.*

Septuagint: *The Greek translation of the Hebrew Old Testament from around 225 B.C.*

Sexual identity: *Understood in relation to politically correct categories, gender identity is subjectively chosen by a person presupposing their personal autonomy.*

Sine qua non: *Latin, "the all or nothing;" refers to that which is indispensable.*

Special Revelation: Holy Scripture; the written text of the Bible—"What Scripture says, God says; for, in a manner comparable only to the deeper mystery of the Incarnation, the Bible is both fully human and fully divine" (J.I. Packer).

Strawman argument: *A logical fallacy wherein an antagonist misrepresents his opponent's position, point of view or argument for the purpose of more easily striking it down.*

Glossary of Terms

Tolerance: *In politically correct categories, tolerance means that when the secular, liberal way of life is in control of the public square, all opposing views to the liberal agenda are viewed as intolerant and extremist and therefore, they must be restricted to the private sphere—politically correct tolerance is an enemy of the 1st Amendment.*

Transgender: *Transgender is the term given to someone whose gender identity does not represent their biological gender. That is, transgender is a person who was either born male but feels like a female; or born female but feels like a male.*

Transsexual: *Transsexual people identify with the opposite gender of their birth. The transsexual person is one who has elected "gender reassignment" surgery and hormone therapy.*

Transphobia: *A term applied to someone who has an aversion to or fear of transgender or transsexual people.*

Transracial: *Presupposes race is simply a "social construct" and therefore, racial appropriation on the outside is based on how a person identifies themselves on the inside.*

Transcendent: *Christian faith believes in a personal God who is beyond physical reality. The personal, transcendent God of the Bible is ultimate reality.*

Triggering: *Commonly used on university campuses to refer to speech that provokes a person's recall of a traumatic experience suffered earlier in life.*

Truth: Christian truth is *not* founded on an impersonal, abstract cosmic principle—*Christian truth is founded on God's revealed Word, both the Incarnation and the Scriptures; and faith, coupled with the Holy Spirit's regeneration and illumination.* Therefore, Biblical authority is at the heart of Christian conviction—*"Sanctify them by the truth; your word is truth"* (Jn. 14:6-7; 18:37; 17:17).

Viz.: *That is; namely.*

*"Three things must happen for a moral revolution to occur:
Something that was nearly universally condemned is now
nearly universally celebrated;
That which was celebrated is condemned;
Those who refuse to celebrate are condemned"*

—Theo Hobson.

Introduction—*Please Read*!

UC Berkeley Then . . . 'Freedom Without Posters'

IN THE FALL OF 1964, the free speech movement was birthed on the campus of the University of California, Berkeley. Originally, the free speech movement intended to give students an opportunity to engage in political activism. Diversity among political persuasions (there was no hardline identity like "left" or "right") characterized the beginning of the free speech movement.

At the same time, the hippie movement emerged. Hippies—an "anti-establishment" knockoff of Rousseau's "Bohemian man"—showed up shouting "Make love, not war!" "Drugs, sex, and rock and roll;" and singing, "Let us dance in the sun, wearing flowers in our hair" all in the name of absolute, autonomous freedom. And anyone who attempted to place any restraints on "freedom"—speech or moral actions—was called a "fascist."

Both the free speech and hippie movements were profoundly influenced by four personalities: Allen Ginsberg, Alan Watts, Gary Snyder, and Timothy Leary. The four men longed for a futuristic drug-inspired utopia characterized by unbridled freedom—Everyone would be free from all restraints to enjoy a blissful, hedonistic existence in a drug-induced "reality." But one of the four voices suddenly struck a "rational" note—Ginsberg interrupted everyone's "trip" by remarking to Leary, "But, Tim, somebody must make the posters."[1] Unless someone makes "the posters," those who clamor for a formless, unrestrained freedom will soon be trapped in an insane cycle of nothingness.

---

1. Schaeffer, "The Church at the End of the Twentieth Century," 25.

Introduction—Please Read!
The Created Order: 'Posters' Are Everywhere!

God's revealed character through both special revelation (the Bible) and the natural order (God's creation) was, for our nation's fathers, the foundation upon which freedom is constitutionally established.

Francis Schaeffer's explanation regarding God's revealed character is profoundly clear:

> One of the distinctions of the Judeo-Christian God is that not all things are the same to Him. That at first may sound rather trivial, but in reality it is one of the most profound things one can say about the Judeo-Christian God. He exists; He has a character; and not all things are the same to Him. Some things conform to His character, and some are opposed to His character. This is in clear distinction, for example, from the Hindu or the Buddhist concept of God. To these gods, everything is the same, so that there is no distinction between good and evil, cruelty and non-cruelty, between tyranny and non-tyranny. In such a setting, speaking of inalienable rights or human rights would be meaningless, because to the Hindu or Buddhist the final reality—their concept of God as the all, the everything—would give no voice, no word, as to why anything is bad; why anything is humanness or anything is lack of humanness. In such a setting, human rights are meaningless.[2]

The Biblical God is revealed as holy Trinity—Father, Son, and Holy Spirit. The three persons in the Trinity are distinguished from one another as to their Person. As image bearers of God, human individuals derive personal dignity from their Creator.

But the Trinity also extends meaning to the whole of humanity, for the three Persons of the Trinity are in perfect unity as the One co-eternal, co-existent, and co-equal God.[3] Adam's creation (Genesis 1 and 2) is described in terms of a corporate entity—"Adam here [Genesis 1 and 2] refers not only to a single man named Adam but, as well, to humanity as a whole."[4] A special *connection* exists between God and *all* of humanity—And Paul therefore points to the unity of the whole human race (Acts 17:26).

---

2. Schaeffer, "Christian Faith and Human Rights," 5. Quoted in: Montgomery, *Human Rights & Human Dignity*, 113.

3. For further study of the doctrine of the holy Trinity, please see: McRoberts, *Systematic Theology, Pentecostal Perspectives*, "The Holy Trinity," Taylor, *The Athanasian Creed in the Twentieth Century*; Luther, *The Smalcald Articles*, Part 1, Statement 1.; Kelly, *Early Christian Creeds*; Warfield, *Studies in Tertullian and Augustine*.

4. Kilner, *Dignity and Destiny*, 85.

Introduction—Please Read!

The Biblical God is moral; and the created order, both the natural order and uniquely, humanity as God's image bearers, reflect his moral nature (Rom. 1:19). There is distinction between good and evil, cruelty and non-cruelty, tyranny and non-tyranny in God's creation—God's creation is not without form, "posters" are everywhere, and therefore, "men are without excuse" (Rom. 1:20).

For the framers of the Constitution, e.g., Thomas Jefferson, John Adams, John Hancock, Patrick Henry, Benjamin Franklin—55 delegates in all, though only 39 signed the Constitution—liberty required our thankfulness to God for His goodness. "Can the liberties of a nation be thought secure," wrote Thomas Jefferson, "when we have removed their only firm basis, a conviction in the minds of the people, that these liberties are the gift of God? That they are violated but with his wrath? I tremble for my country when I reflect that God is just, and that His justice cannot sleep forever."[5]

In my first book, *New Age or Old Lie?* I wrote: "The Church's ... confusing godly separation with isolationism is resulting in the turning over of our culture to the ungodly by default."[6] The process of the desecration of God's created order began decades before my first book written thirty years ago (see, Chapter 1 below, especially the conclusion, "A Moral Revolution").

But increasingly, our nation is turning a deaf ear to God's prophetic conscience (*et. al.,* Rom. 13:1-7). With great urgency, the church must intentionally be for our nation what it cannot be for itself.[7] The American church's vocation is to be "salt" and "light" for a nation that increasingly defiantly refuses to acknowledge God, and neither is it thankful.

America's cultural survival—especially the restoration of sanity and civility—requires a spiritual solution: the church's worshipful acknowledgement of God through her public incarnation of Jesus' Sermon on the Mount. Towards this end, this book is concerned with three primary motifs:

1. Lawless Insanity: A Harvard student, speaking at his commencement, acutely described the lawless [insane] times in which we live: "*The freedom of our day is the freedom to devote ourselves to any values we please, on the mere condition that we do not believe them to be true.*"[8] Lawlessness is not saying, "I know this is wrong, but I'm going to do

---

5. Waldstreicher, ed., *Notes on the State of Virginia*. Quoted in: Guinness, *A Free People's Suicide, Sustainable Freedom and the American Future*, 117.

6. McRoberts, *New Age or Old Lie?* 127.

7. *Response*, Seattle Pacific University, "A Conversation with N.T. Wright."

8. Kuehne, *Sex and the I-World: Rethinking Relationship in an Age of Individualism*, 43.

Introduction—Please Read!

it anyway," rather lawlessness is saying, *"Who's to say what right and wrong is?"*

2. Cultural Transformation: *If, beginning on the cultural margins, the Sermon on the Mount takes narrative form in a minority of God's covenant people, lawless insanity in local communities will be countered—"It is living-in-truth that proves culturally powerful."*[9]

3. Acknowledging God: *The single, most pressing vision of this book is our nation's renewed acknowledgement of God and the consequent restoration of sanity and civility to our culture.*

In the Sermon on the Mount, Jesus' divine wisdom addresses every contemporary issue that is the source of our nation's division and potential downfall—*The issues that most trouble our nation are moral issues; and every issue is traceable to what it means to be human.* But before we engage in our extended study of American culture, the Sermon on the Mount, and the restoration of sanity and civility to our nation, we will return to Berkeley.[10]

UC Berkeley Now . . . 'Freedom Without Posters'

In 2017, Milo Yiannopoulos, a conservative editor of Breitbart News, was scheduled to speak against "sanctuary campuses"[11] at the University of California, Berkeley.[12] Yiannopoulos' speech was scheduled in the wake of President Trump's tough stance on illegal immigration.

Students were not the only ones to object to Yiannopoulos coming to the university, several faculty members urged the Chancellor to cancel the event: *"Although we object strenuously to Yiannopoulos's views—he advocates white supremacy, transphobia, and misogyny—it is rather his harmful conduct to which we call attention in asking for the cancellation of this event,"* read the first of two letters from faculty members.

---

9. Guinness, *Renaissance, The Power of the Gospel However Dark the Times*, 75.

10. I am in Glen Stassen's debt for his method of interpreting the Sermon on the Mount. I have slightly modified Dr. Stassen's observed threefold pattern to the interpretation of the Sermon on the Mount. Please see: Glen Stassen & David Gushee, *Kingdom Ethics*, 142.

11. *"Sanctuary Campuses,"* promise to protect "undocumented students" (the quotes point the politically correct designation for illegal aliens). Yiannopoulos' events are "in your face" crude and obnoxious. I am not commending Yiannopoulos' events to anyone, I am simply advocating free speech as "a two-way street."

12. "Riots Break Out at UC Berkeley Amid Protests of Breitbart Editor's Speech."

Introduction—Please Read!

The protests against Yiannopoulos' "anti-immigration" speech among UC students and faculty quickly turned violent and the event was swiftly cancelled. The cancellation of the event, however, did nothing to temper violence—protestors tore down barricades, lit fires, threw rocks and smashed windows. Not only was there extensive property damage, there were reports of outbreaks of physical violence and rioters intimidating attendees to Yiannopoulos' event as they called them *"fascists."*

Several UC faculty (reportedly more than 100) blamed Yiannopoulos for provoking "incitement, harassment, and defamation." This indictment may, on the surface, appear ironic for Berkeley was the birthplace of the free speech movement and now, they are violently reacting to free speech on their campus. But the University of California has been consistently inconsistent. Berkeley, caught up in a vicious cycle of insanity, has come full circle from the '60s—No one ever bothered "to make the posters"—Absolute unbridled (autonomous) freedom, that is, freedom without any restraints, without any form or outside Transcendent or Absolute to guide it will inevitably "lead in the direction of an establishment totalitarianism."[13]

The Berkeley protesters, when left to themselves, end up creating the very thing they are protesting, viz., fascism. Freedom "without posters," that is, freedom without form means the created order is an end itself, there is nothing outside the created order to distinguish freedom from anarchy, order from chaos, righteousness from unrighteousness—fallen humanity becomes their own end, their own moral-standard, their own god. This notion moved the late postmodern philosopher, Michael Foucault, to lament, "the only freedom is insanity."[14]

---

13. Schaeffer, "The Church at the End of the Twentieth Century," 25.
14. Ibid., 11.

Chapter 1

Insanity!

BABYLON'S KING, NEBUCHADNEZZAR, DREAMED of his pending insanity: *"Let his mind be changed from that of a man and let him be given the mind of an animal. . . ."* And *". . . you will eat grass like the ox and be drenched with the dew of heaven. . . ."* (Dan. 4:16; 25a). What was the source of Nebuchadnezzar's insanity? And how could the king's sanity be restored? All of Babylon's "wise men," magicians, enchanters, astrologers and diviners were summoned by the king to come before him and interpret his dream, but none of them could interpret the dream.

Finally, the king called for Daniel to interpret his dream, and the prophet of Israel's God said to the king: *". . . until you acknowledge that the Most High is sovereign over all kingdoms on earth and gives them to anyone he wishes, your sanity will not be restored"* (Dan. 4:25b; 34–37).

America's Nearly Universal Celebration of The Perversion of The Created Order

Voltaire's pithy remark penetrates the depths of human depravity: "If God has made us in his image, we have returned him the favor."[1] "God" is fallen man's autobiography—". . . our created nature enables us to reflect the glory of God in a dependent and finite form, but our fallen nature impels us to appropriate the glory of God in an autonomous [lit. 'self-law'] and infinite

---

1. Voltaire [Francois Marie Arouet]. 1880. *Le Sottisier.* Paris: Librairie des bibliophiles. Quoted in: Kilner, *Dignity and Destiny, Humanity in the Image of God,* 28.

INSANITY!

form"[2]—*Cultural appropriation of the glory of God "in an autonomous and infinite form" inexorably leads to lawlessness, a blurring of the line between right and wrong.*[3]

Romans 1:18-32 is revelation of humanity's pathological descent into idolatry and unnatural,[4] lawless [insane] behavior through their perversion of the created order. John of Damascus eloquently describes (1:19): The "very creation, by its harmony and ordering, proclaims the majesty of the divine nature"[5]—*God's divine attributes are continually being perceived and therefore, concludes Paul: "men are without excuse"*[6] (1:20).

All people have knowledge of God; not merely a vague sense of something beyond themselves but a knowledge grasped from a non-inferential, fundamental knowledge of God, viz., God's divine power, (1:20); a sense of God's natural order or pattern for life, (1:27); and God's moral law (1:32). Thus, virtually ". . . all the wisdom we possess, that is, true and sound wisdom, consists of two parts: the knowledge of God and of ourselves."[7] But in-spite of what he knows, fallen humanity chooses "to suppress" [or better, "repress"[8]] the truth" (1:18). What truth does fallen humanity choose to repress? The truth that "our very being is nothing but subsistence in the one God."[9] But because fallen man refuses to acknowledge God, his thinking becomes "futile"—he thinks about worthless things[10]—and his senseless heart is darkened (1:21).

In the 1960s Western civilization's shared common values were exchanged for social ideas advanced by the vain philosophies of godless

---

2. Alexander, "Occult Philosophy and Mystical Experience," 17.

3. Colson, *Colson Speaks*, 179. Colson delivered this speech at the Harvard Business School, April. 1991. Charles Colson spoke of the classic work of the historian, Paul Johnson, *Modern Times*. In the 1920s and 1930s fixed assumptions of Western civilization, by which people lived for twenty-three centuries—a set of fixed and shared common values guided by a transcendent value system, were being challenged by people.

4. The meaning of "nature" by Paul in Romans 1 is a focus of a discussion on "Same-Sex Marriage" contained in Chapter 5, Marriage and Divorce.

5. John of Damascus, FC 37:166.

6. Re: Romans 1:20, the "invisible things;" e.g., God's power and moral law *are clearly seen* (present passive indicative) and they are, *"Being perceived"*—present passive participle.

7. Calvin, *Institutes of the Christian Religion*, I.i.1.

8. BAGD, *A Greek-English Lexicon of the New Testament*, 422.

9. Calvin, *Institutes of the Christian Religion*, I.i.1.

10. BAGD., 495.

men;[11] among them were Albert Camus and Jean-Paul Sartre. In 1947, Albert Camus' comments to the assembled student body of Columbia University echoed Paul's description of humanity's descent into idolatry—1:22-23[12]: "There is nothing."[13] Camus' nihilism concluded that there is no transcendent [religious] value; life is meaningless and the only way we can discover any purpose for living is if we overcome life's nothingness with "heroic individualism"[14]—Camus' futile thinking drove him to conclude that the purpose of life is to discover personal peace and meaning through [our] own autonomous efforts.

Today, Camus' "heroic individualism" is recast in the mold of a "hyper-modernism." Hyper-modernism is unbridled human autonomy—"limitless individualism and freedom from social obligations and structuring conventions are finally fulfilled" through humanities' social evolution[15]—*That is, there are no posters; creation is formless and without meaning; we are alone in the universe to do whatever is right in our own eyes.*

Any notion of transcendent truth [God's character revealed in Scripture or in the created order] is regarded too restrictive—human dignity and moral/ethical reflection submit to man's pursuit of absolute autonomous freedom. The human distinction [our special creation in God's image] disappears along with the disappearance of the sacred[16] [that is, humanity's refusal to acknowledge God, 1:18; 21; 28].

---

11. Camus and Sartre were atheistic existentialists. Fundamentally, "existentialism" is a philosophy about *existence*. Existentialism defines human nature by our moral motions, that is, the choices we make—Sartre said: "I am my choices." To be a "self-made" man or woman is to have created one's nature and value through their choices. Whereas there is truth in existentialism, it is half-truth; in other words, we are free moral agents but our moral nature is part of our special creation in the image of a personal, living God. Therefore, the choices we make say something about our character but not our origins, that is, we are not creating our nature through our choices, we are rather expressing our nature.

12. Romans 1:22-23:*"Although they claimed to be wise, they became fools and exchanged the glory of the immortal God for images made to look like mortal man and birds and animals and reptiles."*

13. Colson, *Colson Speaks*, 179.

14. Ibid.

15. Kirby, "Successor States To An Empire In Free Fall." The term "hypermodern" originates with a French philosopher, Gilles Lipovetsky. Other theories related to hyper-modernity include: Raoul Esheman's "performatism;" Robert Samuels' "automodernity," and Alan Kirby's "digimodernism."

16. For outstanding insight regards this discussion, please see: Sommerville, *The Decline of the Secular University*, 23-38.

INSANITY!

Our nation's narcissistic view of human freedom conflates subjective relativism—good and evil are purely subjective and therefore relative to personal evaluation: "Is it good *to* me? Is it evil or wrong *to* me?" And absolute human autonomy—individualism is limitless; there are no boundaries for human behavior and therefore, there are no restrictions or "sacred limits" on the way we treat one another.[17] As the profane is unleased, lawlessness, disguised as freedom, is free to pervert the natural order and everything formerly considered sacred, especially the value of a human being.

A Harvard student, speaking at his commencement, acutely described the lawless times in which we live: *"The freedom of our day is the freedom to devote ourselves to any values we please, on the mere condition that we do not believe them to be true."*[18] Lawlessness is not saying, "I know this is wrong, but I'm going to do it anyway," rather lawlessness is saying, *"Who's to say what right and wrong is?"*

The inherent value of justice—the true, intrinsic value of justice—relates to the ultimate truths we, as a society, ought to live by, and how our beliefs should be related to public life.[19] Justice under the law, like all things virtuous, requires sacred limits—limits imposed by our awareness of that which "we might not be able to 'explain,'"[20] that is, our non-inferential [unexplained] fundamental acknowledgement of human dignity.

However, questions regarding the inherent value of justice and ultimate truth to live by simply do not surface from within the cultural chaos created by lawlessness—lawlessness creates societal conditions wherein the notion of "legal" or "justice" is conformed to the "fiction-driven-narrative" of the lawless: In a progressive/postmodern context, the narrative a group, community or movement creates for their identity or proposed social or political purpose is their own private "reality" or "truth."

The loss of transcendence (that is, our refusal to acknowledge God); and the resulting disappearance of the sacred (the inherent value of human dignity) will ultimately result in the death of our culture.

Three times Paul says, God "gave them over"—"Therefore God gave them over in the sinful desires of their hearts to sexual impurity for the degrading of their bodies with one another;" "Because of this, God gave them over to shameful lusts;" "Furthermore, since they did not think it worthwhile

---

17. Ibid., 34.
18. Kuehne, *Sex and the I-World*, 43.
19. Guinness, *The Case for Civility*, 184.
20. Sommerville, *Decline of the Secular University*, 34.

INSANITY!

to retain the knowledge of God, he gave them over to a depraved mind to do what ought not to be done," re: 1:24, 26, and 28—"They were given over, not so they could do what they did not want to do, but so they could carry out exactly what they desired . . . ."[21] "God gave them over" to both a debased mind and behavior—"The words sound to us like clods on the coffin as God leaves men to work their own wicked will."[22]

While our cities burn, and businesses are looted, criminals are memorialized as fallen heroes. And while the police are ordered to stand down, they are assaulted with bricks and stones and in the aftermath of the mayhem, they stand trial as suspects.

Daily, our "post-human"[23] culture is confronted with a staggering degree of moral and ethical distortion: abortion-on-demand and Planned Parenthood's barbaric harvesting of the organs of the unborn—and yet, those who expose such evil are condemned instead of the reapers of babies' insides; the sex-trafficking industry's wretched desecration of human dignity, physician assisted suicide, genetic engineering, the casting aside of the Tenth Amendment for an unconstitutional judicial edict to make same-sex marriage the law of the land,[24] incessant charges of racism, many painfully true but too many for the purpose of political/social manipulation; widespread municipal, state and federal political corruption; pedophilia among Roman Catholic clergy and adultery among Protestant clergy—The exposed subscribers to the "Ashley Madison" website included "several hundred ministers and church leaders in various denominations from across America;"[25] deadly shootings in schools, the market place, bars and sanctuaries—everywhere we live, work and worship; Islamic extremists and also domestic terrorists; illegal immigration and sanctuary cities where repeat felons are safe but not law-abiding citizens—business owners,

---

21. Ambrosiaster, *Commentary on Paul's Epistles,* 81.47. Quoted in: Witherington III, *Paul's Letter to the Romans,* 68–69.

22. Robertson, *Word Pictures In The New Testament,* 330.

23. "Post-human" is Johns Hopkins University professor, Francis Fukuyama's term: *Our Post-Human Future, Consequences of the Biotechnology Revolution.* Please see: Chapter Three, "Murder" and the subtopic, "The Sacredness of Human Life" for a discussion of what it means to be human.

24. Please see: Appendix 1, "Same Sex Marriage" for a discussion of this point.

25. The "Ashley Madison" website, a service committed to producing adulterous affairs, was compromised by hackers resulting in the exposure of the website's client list. Don Ross, Network Leader, Northwest Ministry Network of the Assemblies of God, Letter dated: September 3, 2015.

florists, bakers and photographers, are "legally" threatened with the loss of their business, home and savings because their conscience based decision (*re*: "Religious Liberty") not to endorse same-sex marriage[26] is trumped by an activist-driven, politically correct "legal" application of discrimination (*re*: 1:29-31).[27]

Our culture's appropriation of the glory of God "in an autonomous and infinite form" means not only our refusal to acknowledge God, but the dishonoring and desecration of human dignity. We not only nearly universally celebrate our perversion of the natural order of God's creation, we also "approve"—although the pagan knows God disapproves of such evil, they give "hearty approval"[28]—of others who participate in such perversions, *re*: 1:32.[29]

'A Moral Revolution'[30]

Herbert Marcuse was a member of the so-called Frankfurt School, a movement formed in Germany during the inter-war period and dedicated to social change. In his essay, "Repressive Tolerance," Marcuse wrote:

> The small and powerless minorities which struggle against the false consciousness and its beneficiaries must be helped: their continued existence is more important than the preservation of abused rights and liberties which grant institutional powers to those who oppress these minorities.[31]

Classical Marxism focused on class conflict, the struggle between the bourgeoisie and the proletariat, the "haves" and the "have nots." Cultural

---

26. See Appendix for discussion of why Christians *are not* demeaning homosexual persons by opposing same-sex marriage.

27. Romans 1:29-31—*29 They have become filled with every kind of wickedness, evil, greed and depravity. They are full of envy, murder, strife, deceit and malice. They are gossips, 30 slanderers, God-haters, insolent, arrogant and boastful; they invent ways of doing evil; they disobey their parents; 31 they have no understanding, no fidelity, no love, no mercy.*

28. BAGD, 788. A.T. Robertson, *Word Pictures In The New Testament*, 333.

29. Romans 1:32—*32 Although they know God's righteous decree that those who do such things deserve death, they not only continue to do these very things but also approve of those who practice them.*

30. Re: "Three things must happen for a moral revolution to occur: Something that was nearly universally condemned is now nearly universally celebrated; That which was celebrated is condemned; Those who refuse to celebrate are condemned"—Theo Hobson. In: Dreher, "America: From Israel to Babylon."

31. Wolff II, Moore Jr., Marcuse, *A Critique of Pure Tolerance*, 110.

Marxism is concerned with social conflict, the struggle between the oppressors and the oppressed; those who are privileged and those who are not.

Because the freeing of the struggling "small and powerless minorities," the oppressed, is a greater social end than the empowerment of the "institutional powers," the oppressors, cultural Marxism calls for the questioning and redefinition of every norm or standard in society, whether it be gender, sexual orientation, family, race, culture or religion, every notion related to a person's identity is to be challenged.[32]

Therefore, majorities, e.g., heterosexuals, whites, especially males, and Christians are oppressive. Those who do not match these descriptions, are the oppressed. So, if heterosexuals are the oppressors, those in the LGBTQ community are the oppressed; if white people are the oppressors, then racial diversity must become a social solution and if Christians are oppressive, the propagation of Islam is then a necessary political end.

Any point of view that differs from cultural Marxism is viewed as a "phobia." If, for example, a resident in London is uncomfortable with a growing, isolated, thoroughly enculturated Muslim community replacing his or her neighborhood, they are "Islamophobic." However, because the Muslims residing in the isolated, thoroughly Islamic and consequently, unassimilated community, are in the category of the oppressed, they are then celebrated for their multiculturalism.

Cultural Marxism makes "Tolerance" an end-in-itself.[33] That is, truth [tolerance] is defined as any view that conforms to the goals of cultural Marxism and any nonconformity, no matter how slight, is viewed as intolerable and consequently, it is condemned, sometimes in the form of violent "protests."

Political Correctness is a popular progressive expression of this view. Political Correctness is committed to the redefinition of Western Civilization by means of questioning common terms and language. For example, "illegal immigrants" are redefined as "undocumented migrants;" ethnic discrimination is called, "affirmative action" and racism and sexism are redefined as prejudice plus power. Therefore, since men are the oppressors, that is, they are the powerful, there is no such thing as "sexism" against men. Only women, regardless of race, are objects of sexism. And, of course, white men cannot be discriminated against, only minorities are victims of racism.

---

32. What is Cultural Marxism? European-Unity.
33. Marcuse, "Repressive Tolerance," 82.

INSANITY!

By redefining terms and language, the far-left controls discourse and alters Western civilization even to the extreme of exchanging that which was formerly nearly universally condemned for what is now nearly universally celebrated—i.e., *The almost total desecration of the created order* (*et. al.*, Romans 1:18-32).

In the same way the desecration of the created order has led to the legalization of abortion-on-demand and gay marriage, we will soon see the legalization and normalizing of ". . . polyamory, polygamy, pedophilia and incest."[34] And those who refuse to celebrate, viz., those whose descent is conscience-based, that is, those whose descent is founded on religious liberty, "are condemned." Those on the far-left, post-Christian liberals, now see Islam—an "oppressed minority"—as means "to rout the vestiges of Judaism and the Christian faith that still stand in their way."[35]

How can the church not just survive but thrive in an increasingly lawless, post-Christian culture? How can the church actively restore sanity to our culture's public discourse?

---

34. Guinness, *Renaissance, The Power of the Gospel However Dark the Times*, 20.
35. Ibid., 19.

Chapter 2

'A Unique Understanding of the Time of the End'

How did the primitive church understand *reality* as citizens of the kingdom of heaven? Gordon Fee points to the daily conscious awareness of the earliest disciples of Jesus Christ: "Probably the one feature that distances the New Testament church the most from its contemporary counterpart is its thoroughly eschatological perspective of all of life. In contrast to most of us, eschatology—a unique understanding of the time of the End—conditioned the early believers' existence in every way."[1]

What is the kingdom of heaven? How does the Gospel relate to the kingdom of heaven? And how does a "unique understanding of the time of the End" condition the thinking and lives of believers?

'The Kingdom of Heaven

In the beginning of the "End," God in human flesh entered the flow of history announcing: *"Repent, for the kingdom of heaven is near"* (Jn. 1:1; 14/ Mt. 4:17). The "kingdom of heaven" (Mark's and Luke's references to the "kingdom of God" are synonymous with Matthew's "kingdom of heaven") refers to God's reign embodied in Jesus.

In the hearing of a conscientious Jewish person living in the Second Temple Period in Palestine, Jesus' proclamation of the nearness of the "kingdom of heaven" related to three outstanding themes: God's chosen

---

1. Fee, *God's Empowering Presence*, 803.

INSANITY!

people were no longer in exile; their sins were forgiven, and Yahweh has returned to renew his covenant with Israel (et. al., Isa. 40-55).[2]

Jesus is Yahweh's representative and through his resurrection, the Son of Man has restored Israel from exile. God's wrath, because of Israel's sins, has been averted through Messiah's death and Yahweh has returned to his people to renew his covenant, not only with Israel, but all nations.

In Genesis 12:1-3, God sovereignly calls Abram into covenant relationship, that is, a mutually binding relationship between two parties who willingly promise to faithfully live by its terms (cf. Deut. 28-29; Lev. 26): *The Lord had said to Abram, "Go from your country, your people and your father's household to the land I will show you. ² "I will make you into a great nation, and I will bless you; I will make your name great, and you will be a blessing. ³ I will bless those who bless you, and whoever curses you I will curse; and all peoples on earth will be blessed through you."*

The primary purpose of God's covenant with Abram was the reversal of the effects of the Fall of humanity (Gen. 3:1-21). The account of God's covenant with Abram begins with God promising an unbelieving, childless Abram that he would bless him with offspring equal in number to the stars in the sky (Gen. 15:1-5).

Abram was 99 years-old and his barren wife, Sarai, was 90 years-old. But Abram believed God, "and he credited it to him as righteousness"[3] (Gen. 15:6).

Ancient covenants required the weaker party to prepare and offer a blood sacrifice to the stronger party. Therefore, after promising to give Abram land as his inheritance (Gen. 15:7), God tells him to bring him a heifer, a goat and a ram each three-years-old along with a dove and a young pigeon (Gen. 15:9).

Abram brought the sacrifice to God and cut each of the larger animals in-half and arranged them opposite of each other. A bloody path through the sacrificed animals was created. Abram did not cut the birds in-half; he severed their heads and drained their blood, mixing it with the other animals (Gen.15:10).

Birds of prey then came down on the sacrifice, but Abram chased them away (Gen. 15:11). As the sun began to set, Abram fell into a deep

---

2. Wright, *The Resurrection of the Son of God*, 320.

3. Paul quotes Genesis 15:6 in Romans 4:3. The word translated "credited" is used by Paul to mean to: "place to one's account . . . credit something to someone. . ..", BADG, 476. By faith, Abraham was justified, that is, God credited to Abraham's account righteousness by faith.

sleep. And he was covered by a thick, dreadful darkness and the Lord spoke to him, "... for four hundred years your descendants will be strangers in a country not their own and ... they will be enslaved and mistreated there." However, "they will come out with great possessions," and "you will go to your ancestors in peace...." (Gen. 15:12-15).

Now, as the sun has set, and the covering of darkness blankets the land, "a smoking firepot with a blazing torch appeared and passed through the pieces" (Gen. 15:17). Something of unspeakable, staggering significance takes place, the "smoking firepot with a blazing torch"—a symbolic representation of the One who led the enslaved Israelites out of "a country not their own" as a "pillar of cloud by day" and a "pillar of fire by night" (Ex. 13:21)—passes through the sacrifice while Abram is in a deep sleep!

Genesis 15:18a.: *"On that day the Lord made a covenant with Abram . . . ."* It is literally of eternal significance that Abram did not pass through the sacrifice, *only* God passed through. This is confounding to Jewish commentators for ancient covenants required the weaker of the two parties to identify with the sacrificed animals and swear, saying something like, "Lord, if I am not obedient to the stipulations of this covenant, may I become as this sacrifice."[4]

By God passing through the sacrifice, Yahweh was literally taking Abram's place! In other words, God made Himself Abram's *substitute*. And therefore, if Abram, and his descendants—"all nations"—were not obedient to the terms of the covenant *"the Lord made ... with Abram,"* God Himself would become as the slaughtered sacrifice in their behalf!

The uniquely inspired apostle, Paul, tells us that regarding Jews and Gentiles everywhere, *"There is no difference . . ., for all have sinned and fall short of the glory of God"* (Rom. 3:22b-23). *"There is no one righteous, not even one. . ."* (Rom. 3:10).

Without exception, no human being has been obedient to the terms of the covenant God made with Abram and "all nations" for the reversing of the effects of our historic fall (Gen. 3:1-19). All *"have sinned,"* sin is any transgression of or lack of conformity to the law of God. *Instead of obeying God's law, fallen (sinful) humanity chooses to be a law unto themselves.* Deep down, in the secret, hidden levels of human existence, every human being intuitively knows something is wrong; but because of their sinful hearts

---

4. Whereas the language involved with this pronouncement is implied, curses associated with disobedience to divine covenants in the Old Testament are explicitly mentioned in: Leviticus 26:14-35; Deuteronomy 28:15-68; and Malachi 2:2.

(cf. Jer. 17:9), they resist turning to God and his law and instead, they are inclined to be a law unto themselves. Everyone, on some level, struggles with the reality of their fallen condition and separation from God.

The Jewish nation was in exile and under the dominion of a foreign ruler, Rome. To be "in exile" is to be outside the covenant and *cursed*. To be blessed, is to be placed in (or to be renewed in) the covenant and for the focused presence of God to be brought *near* and fill the land and community. *Blessing* and *curse* are related to proximity in the Jewish mind; blessing is related to nearness and curse relates to remoteness.

On a Friday afternoon, outside the gates of Jerusalem, [13]*"Christ redeemed us from the curse of the law by becoming a curse for us, for it is written: 'Cursed is everyone who is hung on a tree.'* [14]*He redeemed us in order that the blessing given to Abraham might come to the Gentiles through Christ Jesus, so that by faith we might receive the promise of the Spirit"* (Gal. 3:13-14).

God in Christ literally became the slaughtered sacrifice for us (*et. al.*, Isa. 52:14-15; 53:4-8). He is our *substitute* and through the blood of the Cross, the curse is broken; God's salvation is a present reality for "all nations," Jews and Gentiles together.

The original thrust of the covenant has been restored, that is, the kingdom of God is universal, it is without boundaries and therefore, it is not culturally contained; salvation is available to "whosoever will" (Jn. 3:16).

God has reclaimed his creation in sovereign power through the Resurrection—the old creation is put to death at Calvary and new creation emerges on Easter Sunday—*The tomb is the womb for new creation!*

How does the Gospel relate to the kingdom of heaven? Jesus is the fulfillment of Jewish hope. The kingdom of God has come, and God's chosen people are no longer in exile,[5] Jews and Gentiles alike now have assurance of the forgiveness of sin.[6] And Yahweh has returned in the person of Jesus of Nazareth to renew his covenant with Israel and restore the full thrust of the covenant to all Gentile nations![7]

The kingdom of heaven, God's universal, sovereign rein was, "actually in process of realization,"[8] in the life and ministry of Jesus. The kingdom of

---

5. Through the Messiah's coming, the Jew is no longer in exile. See, Isaiah: 9:1-7; 24:14—25:12; 26; 31:1—32:20; 35; 42:1—44:8; 49:1-7; 51:1-13; 60:1-3; 61; 62.

6. Jesus, the Messiah, has provided the Jewish nation assurance of the forgiveness of sin. See Isaiah: 4:2-6; 40:1-11; 52:7-10;13-15; 53:12; 59:15-17;19-21; 63:1; 3; 5; 9.

7. Yahweh has returned in the person of Jesus of Nazareth to renew his covenant with Israel. See Isaiah: 49:8-26; 54:9-17; 56; 62:10-11; 63:1, 3,5,9; 64:1.

8. Fee, *Called and Empowered*, Dempster, Klause and Petersen, 8, 10.

'A Unique Understanding of the Time of the End'

heaven is understood as referring to God's dynamic rein as *inaugurated* in and through the Messiah, Jesus of Nazareth.

How does a "unique understanding of the time of the End" condition the thinking and lives of believers? A "unique understanding of the time of the End" sees the present kingdom as the first-fruits of the future kingdom. There is then, "an underlying continuity between present bodily life and future bodily life, and that gives meaning and direction to present Christian living"[9]—*Our daily lives are conditioned by both our connection to Jesus' historical resurrection and our future imperishable, immortal and incorruptible resurrection and that gives ultimate meaning to every ordinary day of our lives* (et. al.,1 Cor. 15:50-57). This understanding of the paradoxical present/future reality of the kingdom of heaven shapes the believer's unique understanding of the End.

How do we, as a new humanity, live in the reality of our future resurrection?

The exaltation themes in the Gospels, specifically Jesus' quoting of Psalm 110:1, identifying himself with the Son of David, and Daniel 7:13-14, relate to the Ascension story, Jesus Christ, the Son of Man, ascends in "the clouds of heaven" and enters the presence of the "Ancient of Days" where he is given "authority, glory and sovereign power" and his dominion will be "an everlasting dominion that will not pass away, and his kingdom is one that will never be destroyed."[10]

The Father and the ascended Son of Man have sent the Holy Spirit (John 14:15-21; 15:26; 16:7-15). The Holy Spirit's work in the time of the End (eschatology) is bringing new creation in place of the old; the whole of creation will experience an exodus, a return from exile through the Spirit's work—*The eschatological work of the Spirit—The Spirit's work in the time of the End,* "conditioned the early believers' lives in every way" *and He continues to condition the lives of believers until the return of our great God and Savior Jesus Christ and the full consummation of the kingdom of heaven* (Titus 2:13/1 Cor. 15:50-57; 1 Thess. 4:13-18). Living in the reality of our future resurrection daily translates into, ". . . *righteousness, peace and joy in the Holy Spirit"!* (Rom. 14:17b).

"The universal witness of the Synoptic tradition is that the absolutely central theme of Jesus' mission and message was 'the good news of the kingdom of God'"[11]—*The present reality of God's unshakeable kingdom is context*

---

9. Wright, *Jesus and the Victory of God,* 643.
10. Ibid.
11. Fee, "The Kingdom of God," 8.

INSANITY!

for a Spirit empowered church's living in the reality of our future resurrection through daily obedience to Jesus' Sermon on the Mount.

Citizenship In The Present/Future Kingdom

The Sermon on the Mount is prefaced by the simplicity and beauty of the Beatitudes. The Beatitudes are "... Christ's own specification of what every Christian ought to be."[12] Jesus is calling us to be a virtuous people; but not in a way that as moral, religious people if we behave, we will be rewarded (a legalistic approach) or, "Now that you've believed in me and my kingdom project, this is how you must behave,"[13] but rather, "Now that I'm here, God's new world is coming to birth; and, once you realize that, you'll see that these are the habits of heart which anticipate that new world here and now."[14] The Beatitudes describe Christ's "ideal for every citizen of God's kingdom"[15] and since the kingdom of heaven is a present/future reality in the life of the believer, we "enjoy the first-fruits now; the full harvest is yet to come."[16]

The setting of Jesus' sermon is described by Matthew 5: [1]*"Now when Jesus saw the crowds, he went up on a mountainside and sat down. His disciples came to him,* [2] *and he began to teach them."*

Jewish teachers sat to expound the scriptures, often with their disciples sitting at their feet. For many commentators, Jesus mirrors an image of Moses on Mount Sinai expounding the law and the unique ethical life of the Jewish nation (Ex. 19-20; *cf.* Isa. 2:2-3).

Matthew tells us Jesus began by saying: [3] *"Blessed are the poor in spirit for theirs is the kingdom of heaven."*

5:3—The "poor in spirit" refers to those who realize their need of total dependence on God. Jesus blesses the poor "... whose sole help is God, not in contrast to those who are rich materially (Lk. 6:20,24) or intellectually but in contrast to those who are rich in religious knowledge and religious achievement."[17]

---

12. Wright, *Jesus and the Victory of God*, 643.
13. Wright, *After You Believe*, 106.
14. Ibid.
15. Stott, *The Message of the Sermon on the Mount*, 31.
16. Ibid., 35.
17. *Theological Dictionary of the New Testament*, Kittel and Friedrich, 401.

Bonhoeffer makes note of those, who "... enjoy greatness and renown, whose feet are firmly planted on the earth, who [are] deeply rooted in the culture and ... molded by the spirit of the age. Yet it is not they, but the disciples who are called blessed, *theirs is the kingdom of heaven.*"[18]

> [4] *Blessed are those who mourn, for they will be comforted.*

5:4—"*Blessed are those who mourn ...*"—"those who mourn" are not merely grieved by their own sin, but the sorrows and sins of others, particularly, in this context, their grief is because of the pain of the oppressed. "'Comfort,' was one of the blessings promised for the future time when God would restore his mourning people (Is 40:1; 49:13; 51:3, 12; 52:9; 54:11; 57:18; 61:2; 66:13)."[19]

> [5] *Blessed are the meek, for they will inherit the earth.*

5:5—"*Blessed are the meek. ...*" (*cf.* Ps. 37:9; 11)—Jesus is not referring to those who, by political or military means, attempt to build the kingdom; but rather he is referring to those who humbly wait for God to bring in the kingdom; they will inherit the earth.

The Greek term translated "meek" means "gentle, humble, considerate ... unassuming."[20] But the word has another connotation, "Wherever the Greek word here translated 'meek' or better, 'humble' ... occurs in the Bible, it always points to peacefulness or peacemaking."[21] Martin Luther King Jr. acknowledges: "Jesus understood the difficulty inherent in the act of loving one's enemy. ... He realized that every genuine expression of love grows out of a consistent and total surrender to God."[22]

> [6] "*Blessed are those who hunger and thirst for righteousness, for they will be filled.*"

5:6—Righteousness and the kingdom are themes central to the Sermon on the Mount.[23] Moral righteousness is characteristic of the man or woman who passionately pursues God's own heart, that is, like David, they are concerned with the things God is concerned with.

18. Bonhoeffer, *The Cost of Discipleship*, 108.
19. Stott and Larsen, *A Deeper Look at the Sermon on the Mount*, 17.
20. BAGD, 698-699.
21. Stassen & Gushee, *Kingdom Ethics*, 40.
22. Luther King Jr., *Strength to Love*, 48.
23. Stassen & Gushee, *Kingdom Ethics*, 41.

INSANITY!

Those who live in the way of Jesus "are longing for the forgiveness of all sin, for complete renewal, for the renewal too of the earth and the full establishment of God's law"[24]—Those who hunger and thirst for the righteousness that God is bringing long for the restoration of "the powerless and the outcasts to their rightful place in covenant community."[25]

[7]*"Blessed are the merciful, for they will be shown mercy."*

5:7—The merciful "have surrendered their hearts completely to Jesus that he may reign in them alone."[26] In all they do, the merciful reflect the image of Jesus Christ in their lives.[27] They are impassioned to help people discover blessing in the middle of pain.

Good times and bad, sorrow and joy are sharply contrasted in our world but in the eyes of God, they are never distinguished. Where pain is, there is also healing; where there is mourning, there is also rejoicing and where there is poverty, there the kingdom of God is manifest.

Ministry, in the heart of the believer, must be to go where the pain is because God is hidden in the pain; the merciful are those who trust that by throwing themselves into the pain they will find the joy of Jesus. All ministry, throughout the history of the church, is built on a vision of *holistic redemption*, that is, the unashamed, single-minded commitment to the Cross and the dynamic presence of the Holy Spirit in the lives of believers, particularly, the merciful.

[8]*"Blessed are the pure in heart, for they will see God."*

5:8—"It is immediately obvious that the words 'in heart' indicate the kind of purity to which Jesus is alluding, as the words 'in spirit' indicated the kind of poverty he meant."[28] The pure in heart are, "the single-minded, who are free from the tyranny of a divided self"[29]: *"Teach me your way, O Lord, and I will walk in your truth; give me an undivided heart, that I may fear your name"* (Ps. 86:11).[30] The pure in heart are unashamedly authentic, they live one life and they live it in the open!

24. Bonhoeffer, *The Cost of Discipleship*, 111.
25. Stassen & Gushee, *Kingdom Ethics*, 42.
26. Bonhoeffer, *The Cost of Discipleship*, 112.
27. Ibid.
28. Stott, *The Message of the Sermon on the Mount*, 48.
29. Ibid.
30. *"The eye is the lamp of the body. If your eyes are good, your whole body will be full*

> ⁹ "Blessed are the peacemakers, for they will be called children of God."

5:9—Through Jesus Christ, God was pleased "to reconcile to himself all things, whether things on earth or things in heaven, by making peace through his blood, shed on the cross" (Col. 1:20). The peacemaker seeks reconciliation; peacemakers *"seek to bring about peace,"*[31] God has called us to live in peace (1 Cor. 7:15); to pursue peace (1 Pt. 3:11); and "If it is possible, as far as it depends on you, live at peace with everyone" (Rm. 12:18). The peacemaker knows the "cost of discipleship" (Bonhoeffer) for he or she is called to "make peace with their enemies, as God shows love to His enemies."[32]

> ¹⁰ "Blessed are those who are persecuted because of righteousness for theirs is the kingdom of heaven."

5:10—Not all peacemaking efforts result in reconciliation. Jesus' transition from the believer as peacemaker to an object of hostility was most outstanding in his life and so it will surely be a reality in the lives of his disciples—*"In fact, everyone who wants to live a godly life in Christ Jesus will be persecuted"* (2 Tim. 3:12).

Although a believer may be slandered, maligned or betrayed because of their love of righteousness, they are not to retaliate like an unbeliever but rather, we are to rejoice—*"The apostles left the Sanhedrin, rejoicing because they had been counted worthy of suffering disgrace for the Name"* (Acts 5:41).

> ¹¹ "Blessed are you when people insult you, persecute you and falsely say all kinds of evil against you because of me."

5:11—We are to rejoice when we are persecuted and when we suffer because of Jesus—"Since all the beatitudes describe what every Christian disciple is intended to be, we conclude that the condition of being despised and rejected, slandered and persecuted, is as much a normal mark of Christian discipleship as being pure in heart or merciful."[33]

---

of light" (Mt. 6:22).

31. Stassen & Gushee, *Kingdom Ethics*, 45.
32. Ibid.
33. Stott, *The Message of the Sermon on the Mount*, 53.

> ¹²*"Rejoice and be glad, because great is your reward in heaven, for in the same way they persecuted the prophets who were before you."*

5:12—In April 1945, Heinrich Himmler, the Reich Leader of the Nazi SS, ordered the execution of Dietrich Bonhoeffer. In the face of death, Bonhoeffer contended: "If we refuse to take up our cross and submit to suffering and rejection at the hands of men, we forfeit our fellowship with Christ and have ceased to follow him. But if we lose our lives in his service and carry our cross, we shall find our lives again in the fellowship of the cross with Christ. The opposite of discipleship is to be ashamed of Christ and his cross and all the offence which the cross brings in its train."

Bonhoeffer continues: "Discipleship means allegiance to the suffering Christ, and it is therefore not at all surprising that Christians should be called upon to suffer. In fact it is a joy and a token of his grace."[34] Therefore, *"Rejoice in that day and leap for joy, because great is your reward in heaven. For that is how their fathers treated the prophets"* (Luke 6:23).

Our Lord is not merely telling us about right beliefs regarding moral behavior; but rather these kingdom virtues "must take on narrative form" in our lives; we are to embody [incarnate] the ethical practices of the kingdom and daily live in a unique understanding of the End.

Kingdom virtues, the "character traits"[35] possessed by Christ's disciples, are framed in Jesus' fulfillment of the Law and the Prophets.

The Law And The Prophets

> **Mt. 5**—¹⁷ *"Do not think that I have come to abolish the Law or the Prophets; I have not come to abolish them but to fulfill them.* ¹⁸ *For truly I tell you, until heaven and earth disappear, not the smallest letter, not the least stroke of a pen, will by any means disappear from the Law until everything is accomplished.* ¹⁹ *Therefore anyone who sets aside one of the least of these commands and teaches others accordingly will be called least in the kingdom of heaven, but whoever practices and teaches these commands will be called great in the kingdom of heaven.* ²⁰ *For I tell you that unless your righteousness surpasses that of the Pharisees and the teachers of the law, you will certainly not enter the kingdom of heaven."*

---

34. Bonhoeffer, *The Cost of Discipleship*, 91.
35. Re: "The spiritual qualities of the disciples," BAGD, 35.

'A Unique Understanding of the Time of the End'

"Do not think. . ." that Jesus' use of six apparent antitheses: "You have heard . . . But I tell you. . ." (Mt. 5:21-22; 27-28; 31-32; 33-34; 38-39; 43-44) suggests that He set aside the Law and chose to ignore Moses.

But what then is the relation between Jesus' and Moses' authority? Does Jesus place himself above the law? It appears that these questions, whether spoken or not, were on people's minds. And therefore, Jesus unequivocally asserts: *"Do not think that I have come to abolish the Law or the Prophets . . . ."* Jesus' identity and authority are founded on his high view of Scripture: *18 For truly I tell you, until heaven and earth disappear, not the smallest letter, not the least stroke of a pen, will by any means disappear from the Law until everything is accomplished."*

There exists no conflict between Jesus and Moses or the prophets.[36] The conflict existed among the teachers of the law who did not speak with Jesus' authority (Mt. 7:29) and neither did they work miracles. They therefore attempted to test him in ways that might result in his contradiction of the law (Mt. 22:15-22) or place him in opposition to the more popular view among the people regarding such things as divorce and remarriage (Mt. 19:3-12).

Jesus, in the tradition of Jewish teachers, used phrases like, *"You have heard . . . but I tell you"* when delivering an exposition of Scripture.[37] Rather than contradicting a former teaching, the Rabbis were providing an explanation. Keener paraphrases: "You understand the Bible to mean only this, but I offer a fuller interpretation."[38]

Jesus acknowledges the full authority of the law; but He is the "decisive arbiter of its meaning."[39] Therefore, "the fulfillment of the law" (Mt. 5:17) prefaces the whole of Jesus' sermon. Kingdom citizens are expected to understand and live-out the moral principles in God's law, *"whoever practices and teaches these commands will be called great in the kingdom of heaven"* (Mt. 5:19b).

"For I tell you that unless your righteousness surpasses that of the Pharisees and the teachers of the law, you will certainly not enter the kingdom of heaven," Jesus is referring to the Mosaic law, the law of the Old Covenant. But now, through faith in Christ, we are bound to a new law. Bonhoeffer

---

36. Davies, and Allison, *A Critical and Exegetical Commentary on the Gospel According to St. Matthew*, 1:481-82, 501. In Stassen & Gushee, *Kingdom Ethics*, 84.
37. Keener, *Matthew*, 113.
38. Ibid.
39. Ibid., 114.

INSANITY!

informs us that for "Christians, therefore, the law is not a 'better law' than that of the Pharisees, but one and the same; every letter of it, every jot and tittle, must remain in force and be observed until the end of the world."[40]

"But," continues Bonhoeffer, "there is a 'better righteousness' which is expected of Christians. Without it none can enter into the kingdom of heaven, for it is the indispensable condition of discipleship. None can have this better righteousness but those to whom Christ is speaking here, those whom he has called. The call of Christ, in fact Christ himself, is the *sine qua non*[41] of this better righteousness."[42]

This "better righteousness" (re: Rom. 1:17) compels the church, the "salt of the earth" (Mt. 5:13), to season and preserve nations and the world. Jesus does not call himself the salt of the earth, but rather his disciples for it is to them that he has entrusted his work. The church is to be the presence of Christ in our culture. The Christian community seasons and preserves culture with their virtuous lives as salt seasons and preserves food; the world is then blessed by the seasoning presence of the church.

---

40. Bonhoeffer, *The Cost of Discipleship*, 121-22.

41. The Latin phrase, *sine qua non*—"the all or nothing" refers to something that is indispensable.

42. Bonhoeffer, *The Cost of Discipleship*, 122.

Chapter 3

The Sermon on the Mount
Living In The Way Of Jesus

Matthew 5:14 – 7:29

Mt. 5—[14] *"You are the light of the world. A town built on a hill cannot be hidden.* [15] *Neither do people light a lamp and put it under a bowl. Instead they put it on its stand, and it gives light to everyone in the house.* [16] *In the same way, let your light shine before others, that they may see your good deeds and glorify your Father in heaven."*

IN THE FIRST THREE centuries of the church, the Sermon on the Mount was regarded as the centerpiece of Jesus' teaching and therefore, it was the primary foundation for Christian formation (discipleship). Throughout the Sermon on the Mount, Jesus expounds on how the radiance of the church (the church's "better righteousness") gives light to the reality of the present kingdom beginning with the 6th Commandment: *"You shall not murder"* (Ex. 20:13). *The sacredness of human life is the single truth upon which everything Jesus says in the Sermon on the Mount is related.*

Murder & The Sacredness Of Life

Matthew 5:21-26

Our vague notions of what it means to be human underlie absolutely every issue—e.g., religious, philosophical, political, racial, economical, educational and the rule of law—in America today.

INSANITY!

Jesus says,

> **Mt. 5—**²¹ *"You have heard that it was said to the people long ago, 'You shall not murder, and anyone who murders will be subject to judgment.'* ²² *But I tell you that anyone who is angry with a brother or sister will be subject to judgment. Again, anyone who says to a brother or sister, 'Raca,' is answerable to the court. And anyone who says, 'You fool!' will be in danger of the fire of hell.*

The teachers of the Law consistently attempted to do less than what the Law required. Consequently, they restricted understanding of the sixth commandment, *"You shall not murder,"* to the act of homicide alone. But Jesus disagreed with their too narrow application of the Law. Instead, Jesus included motives, thoughts, words and deeds. Whereas an earthly court is incapable of judging anger, the heavenly court of God judges the human heart and the offense of anger (Mt. 5:22).

Of course, not all anger is evil. God's wrath is spoken of in Scripture (e.g., Rom. 1:18), and Jesus was angry in the Temple (Mt. 21:12-3). Luther, referring to his own experience of righteous anger, called it "an anger of love, one that wishes no one any evil, one that is friendly to the person but hostile to the sin."[1] Here, in Matthew 5:22, Jesus is referring to an inner sinful rage—hatred, malice, revenge.

At the end of verse 22, Jesus warns us not to slander our brother or sister by calling either one *Raca*—an Aramaean term of contempt (lit.) "empty one," and probably meaning, "empty-head," "numbskull," "fool."[2] *Raca* refers to a person's intelligence.

The second slanderous term in verse 22 Jesus warns us against using to refer to another person is "fool" (Grk., μωρέ). Though the meaning is disputed, a scholarly consensus takes the term to mean, an obstinate, godless person.[3]

Stott points out that the term translated "fool" in verse 22 "had acquired both religious and moral overtones, being applied in the Old Testament to those who denied God's existence and as a result plunged into

---

1. Luther, *The Sermon on the Mount*. In: Stott, *The Message of the Sermon on the Mount*, 84.
2. BAGD, 733.
3. BAGD, 531.

reckless evil doing."[4] Quoting Tasker, Stott concludes: "The man who tells his brother that he is doomed to hell is in danger of hell himself."[5]

Although anger and slander may not result in murder, they are equivalent in God's eyes to murder.[6] Therefore, though the Rabbis may have taught that the sentence imposed on the murderer was judgment in an earthly court, Jesus added that anger and slander ultimately exposes us to divine judgment in the heavenly court and *"the fire of hell."* Keener calls our attention to Jesus' focused concern: "God has never merely wanted people to obey rules; he wants them to be holy as he is, to value what he values."[7] *God values people. And therefore, everything Jesus did and taught in his earthly ministry is founded on who God is and the sacred value of human life.*

What Does It Mean To Be Human?

"The morality of the 21st century will depend on how we respond to this simple but profound question: Does every human life have equal moral value simply because it is human? Answer yes, and we have a chance of achieving universal human rights. Answer no, and it means that we are merely another animal in the forest"—Wesley J. Smith, Senior Fellow, Discovery Institute.[8]

Does every human life have equal moral value simply because it is human?

Traditional assessments of what it means to be human have been banished from the public square, especially in the classroom of the modern university. Never-the-less, the different schools in the university system depend on some notion, or ideal, of what it means to be human. The School of Business is concerned with creating well-being, or "wealth" and The School of Psychology is concerned with notions of human sanity or insanity. The School of Anthropology is concerned with human origins and The Law School presupposes human morality. The School of Fine Arts is concerned with human creativity and until recently, Medical School graduates

---

4. Stott, *The Message of the Sermon on the Mount*, 84.
5. Tasker, *The Gospel According to St. Matthew*, 107. In Stott, Ibid.
6. Re: 1 John 3:15.
7. Keener, *Matthew*, 114.
8. Smith, "The Human Exceptionalist—July, 2012."

affirmed the words of the Hippocratic Oath, "I will not give a woman a pessary[9] to produce an abortion."[10]

The Sacredness Of Human Life

The Biblical narrative begins with God, on a specific day, the sixth day, personally forming man from clay, the ground of his creation. And God "breathed into his nostrils the breath of life," and the "man became a living being" (Genesis 2:7). The Bible unveils a *normative* understanding of what it means to be human.

The first clause of Genesis 2:7: "*. . . the Lord God formed the man from the dust of the ground . . .*" reveals "that man is part 'dust,' a better word is, 'clay,' personally fashioned by God."[11] Our origins are from the earth (Genesis 2:7a), and upon death, we return to the earth (Ecclesiastes 3:20).

The second clause of Genesis 2:7 continues, "*. . . and breathed into his nostrils the breath of life . . . .*"[12] Human life is animated by God's breath[13]—our origin is not only from the earth but also from heaven.

The third clause—Genesis 2:7c, follows, "*. . . and the man became a living being. . .*" or a "living soul" (Heb. *nephesh*). Genesis 2:7c informs us that rather than "soul" being a distinct part of a person's being (as though we contained a soul), a person is a "living soul," a wholly integrated being—body, spirit/soul. *Therefore, if any part of the body is formed, so also is the spirit/soul.*[14]

9. A "pessary" is a small soluble block inserted into the vagina. Re: Kaiser Jr., *What Does The Lord Require?*", 105.

10. I am here paraphrasing Sommerville's introduction to: "Trouble Defining The Human," *The Decline of the Secular University*, 23.

11. Waltke, "Reflections From The Old Testament On Abortion," delivered as the presidential address at the 27th annual meeting of the Evangelical Theological Society, December 29, 1975.

12. Waltke notes: "I understand the phrase 'of life' to be a subjective genitive denoting that man's breath is a manifestation of life," Ibid.

13. Et. al., "*. . . as long as I have life within me, the breath of God in my nostrils . . .*" - Job 27:3; *"If it were his intention and he withdrew his spirit and breath, all mankind would perish together and man would return to the dust"* - Job 34:14-15; "*. . . and the dust returns to the ground it came from, and the spirit returns to God who gave it*" - Eccl. 12:7; Isa. 42:5 - "*This is what God the Lord says - he who created the heavens and stretched them out, who spread out the earth and all that comes out of it, who gives breath to its people, and life to those who walk on it:. . .*"

14. This distinguishes between a Biblical view of man and the Greek view, i.e., "the

Genesis 2:7 clearly reveals the origins of life; and Genesis 1:26-27 is revelation of human dignity, that is, the nature of humanity: [26] *Then God said, "Let us make mankind in our image, in our likeness, so that they may rule over the fish in the sea and the birds in the sky, over the livestock and all the wild animals, and over all the creatures that move along the ground."* [27] *So God created mankind in his own image, in the image of God he created them; male and female he created them.*

As image bearers of God, we are distinguished from "merely another animal in the forest." We are created in His "likeness" and "image." The Hebrew text of Genesis 1:26 speaks of a distinct divine likeness: The "likeness-image" tells us that the image in view relates to, or is somehow like the original.[15] The "likeness-image" of God "involves humanity's special *connection* with God, which makes it possible for humanity to be a meaningful *reflection* of God."[16] Kierkegaard then concludes that the relationship between God and man (the "likeness-image") is what makes man a man.[17]

God is the source and foundation for human existence, male and female identity, as sexual creatures, is distinctively, and communally, especially through marriage, reflected in our special creation in God's image (*re:* verse 27).

Moreover, Adam's creation (Genesis 1 and 2) is described in terms of a corporate entity: *"Adam* here refers not only to a single man named Adam but also to humanity as a whole."[18]

In Acts 17:26, Paul embraces this divine reality in what is Biblically "the unity of the human-race." To the Athenians, Paul proclaimed: *"God has made from one all nations of men to dwell on the face of the whole earth."* God *directly* gave Adam life when he breathed into him; and the life breathed into Adam is then passed on seminally, and is present at the time of conception.[19] We conclude, from the doctrine of the unity of the human-race, that *all* of humanity is created in the image of God; a special *connection* exists between God and *all* of humanity. The inherent value of

---

body is the prison house of the soul." This distinction has profound implications for Christian ethics, to be discussed later in this book.

15. Kilner, *Dignity and Destiny*, 128, 129
16. Ibid., 114.
17. Kierkegaard, *The Point of View*, 114.
18. Kilner, *Dignity and Destiny*, 85.
19. Waltke, "Reflections from The Old Testament On Abortion," 11.

INSANITY!

every human being: red, black, yellow, brown and white, as an image bearer of God, is the foundation for individual human dignity.

But when do we become human? Is there a duration of time in our prenatal development when, regards our humanness, we are indistinguishable from "... another animal in the forest"?

By redefining what it means to be human in a way that excludes the unborn, we have made room for our wretchedness to conclude the unborn are not "endowed by their Creator with certain unalienable Rights." [20] But our special creation in the image of God—*even from the very moment of our prenatal existence*—is evidence of our humanness: God created our inmost being (Ps. 139:13a); God shaped each of us in our mother's womb (Ps. 139:13b-14); God saw our embryo[21]—"*God's eyes ... saw my unformed body*" (Ps. 139:16a);[22] and He loved each one of us (Ps. 139:15-16a); and God ordained all of our days before we were born—Psalm 139:17-18: *[17] How precious to me are your thoughts, God! How vast is the sum of them! [18] Were I to count them, they would outnumber the grains of sand—when I awake, I am still with you. . . ."*[23]

The unborn is fashioned by God in ways that are like Adam. But, unlike Adam, the Scripture does not teach that the life of the baby comes *directly* from God but rather, *instrumentally* from the child's parents through the seminal process. This is inferred in Genesis 2:2 where the Scripture informs us that God ceased from his creative work on the seventh day[24]: *[2] "By the seventh day God had finished the work he had been doing; so on the seventh day he rested from all his work;"* and also, Genesis 1:28, wherein God gives the gift of reproduction to us, his creation: *"God blessed them and said to them, 'Be fruitful and increase in number . . . .'"*

---

20. Nazi Germany, under Hitler's control, redefined Jews as less than human for justification of the Third Reich's extermination of the Jewish race. Hitler, *Mein Kampf*.

21. Within twelve hours of sexual intercourse, the egg nucleus and the sperm nucleus fuse together, Meyers, *Psychology*, 9th ed., 140. In: Gushee, *The Sacredness of Human Life*, 357-358.

22. The Hebrew word translated, "my embryo" is *golmi*. Kaiser notes that this "Hebrew word is used since the embryo is in the shape of an egg . . . ." Kaiser continues stating, "... the word 'embryo,' means 'to roll, to wrap together,' just as the Latin word *glomus* means a 'ball,' *What Does the Lord Require?* 111-112.

23. Cf. Job 10:8-12.

24. Waltke, "Reflections from The Old Testament On Abortion," 11.

The Bible clearly teaches that in the moment of conception, humanity's sinful nature (*re: the doctrine of original sin*[25]) which is related to his spiritual, moral nature, is passed on seminally through the reproductive process to the baby—*The Scripture unequivocally establishes the fact that the moral nature of a human is in place at the precise moment of conception.*[26]

Moreover, Genesis 5:3 says, "*When Adam had lived 130 years, he had a son in his own likeness, in his own image . . .*"—Adam "fathered" a son. The Bible clearly intends to assert that the essential feature of humanness, that which relates humankind to God, that is, the image of God, is transferred through the reproductive process—the image of God is seminally passed down—*Both human life and personality are present at the precise moment of conception.*[27]

Martin Luther King Jr. rightly contended, ". . . there are no gradations in the image God"[28]—*The baby is fully in the image of God at conception.* Therefore, the Bible *always* refers to the unborn as a "baby" or a "child"— e.g., Ex. 21:22, Matt.1:25; Isa. 7:14; Lk. 1:41; 44. "Clearly," observes Kaiser, "the work and care of our Lord went all the way back to our being originally formed in the womb. God himself did not think that the embryo was 'just so much tissue,' and not a living being; on the contrary, his love and affection were placed on us even as we were being stitched together in our mother's womb."[29]

The primitive church was known for its opposition to abortion and infanticide contrary to the immoral, degenerated Greco-Roman culture where these practices were widespread. For example, Clement of Alexandria (150-215 A.D.) forcibly proclaimed: "Our whole life can proceed according to God's perfect plan only if we gain dominion over our desires, practicing continence from the beginning instead of destroying through perverse and pernicious arts human offspring, who are given birth by Divine Providence. Those who use abortifacient medicines to hide their

---

25. Rom. 5:12; 15-19/Ps. 51:5.

26. Waltke; particularly, Ps. 51:5.

27. Waltke notes: "The verb *holid* everywhere else means to 'father a child,'" re: Brown, Driver, and Briggs, *A Hebrew and English Lexicon*, 409. Waltke concludes: "Without doubt, then, the author intends his reader to understand that through sexual intercourse - seminally - the essential feature of humanness, that which relates man to God and separates him from the rest of nature, is handed down," Ibid.,12.

28. Luther King, Jr. 1965, "The American Dream." In: *Dignity and Destiny,* 97.

29. Kaiser, *What Does The Lord Require?* 112.

INSANITY!

fornication cause not only the outright murder of the fetus, but of the whole human race as well."[30]

A society is only as just and free as it holds sacred the unalienable right to life of its citizens, especially the lives of its most vulnerable[31]—*If the unborn are in the image of God in the very moment of conception then, any attempt to dehumanize the unborn, from the precise moment of conception to full-term, ultimately results in the dehumanizing of ourselves as a nation.*[32]

Living In The Way Of Jesus

> **Mt. 5**—[23] *"Therefore . . . go and be reconciled . . ."* A kingdom ethic seeks to prevent violence and preserve all human life, as our Father in heaven wills (Mt. 5:45,48). Jesus' teaching here is very clear: We are our "brother's keeper"—*A kingdom ethic seeks always to preserve another's dignity; to include [especially] our enemy.* In this context, Jesus is not only referring to relationships among believers—[23] *"Therefore, if you are offering your gift at the altar and there remember that your brother or sister has something against you,* [24] *leave your gift there in front of the altar. First go and be reconciled to them; then come and offer your gift*—but obedience to a kingdom ethic means that there are no limits on who our neighbor may be (*et. al.*, Lk. 10:25-37).

Therefore, [25] *"Settle matters quickly with your adversary who is taking you to court. Do it while you are still together on the way, or your adversary may hand you over to the judge, and the judge may hand you over to the officer, and you may be thrown into prison.* [26] *Truly I tell you, you will not get out until you have paid the last penny."*

---

30. Clement of Alexandria, *Paedagogus*, 2.10.96.1. In: Kaiser, *What Does The Lord Require?* 107.

31. Physician assisted suicide—*active euthanasia*—follows from abortion-on-demand: If life is without inherent value before birth, the physically or mentally dysfunctional; terminal or severely disabled, the elderly—*life on the other end of pre-birth, is without inherent value.*

32. I acknowledge that exceptions to the preserving of the life of the unborn need to be discussed. If the life of the mother, because of an ectopic pregnancy for example, is in jeopardy, although the aborting of the unborn involves the killing of a human being, the saving of the mother's life is, if you will, a matter of "self-defense." But apart from the preserving of the mother's life, abortion is not Biblically sanctioned. I am, however, constrained to add, in cases of rape and incest, thoughtful, sober debate, in relation to God's revelation and tender consciences, needs to "openly" (civilly) take place.

Rather than worrying about being right and therefore rushing to defend ourselves, we are to make peace with those who are angry with us and are accusing us.

Practically speaking, it is better to first listen and try to understand why your adversary holds their point of view. A kingdom ethic—*the way of Jesus*—is most outstandingly marked by sacrificial love. That is, interpreting and living life by way of the Cross or more plainly, taking the other person's place and relating to their worldview, their understanding reality.[33]

Although Jesus' instructions appear to directly apply to the courtroom, they are logical implications of the sixth commandment that apply in any situation, to include the great divide between pro-life and pro-choice advocates. Regarding a kingdom ethic, the practical understanding is for us to, if possible, *". . . as far as it depends on you, live at peace with everyone"* (Romans 12:18).

A Culture Of Abortion

A disproportionate number of abortions involve poor women and women of color.[34] As may be expected, during times of economic crisis and social unrest, abortion rates increase: "A surprisingly high percentage of abortions are chosen by married women, often because they fear that a pregnancy or (another) child would snap the fragile bonds that keep their marriage and family together or would tax them financially beyond what they can bear. Abortion is quite often a desperate measure for a crisis moment in a woman's life, so that abortion is not an expression of her agency or freedom but of her tragic desperation."[35]

---

33. A *normative* understanding of, in this case, a pro-choice person's point of view, involves reading the primary sources published for a pro-choice point of view—*how do pro-choice advocates define their terms? How do they defend their position? Precisely, what are they really defending?* Rather than what a secondary source, usually a pro-life advocate, tells you what the pro-choice advocate means by their use of certain terms and language; and what they are defending.

34. Gushee notes that: "Non-Hispanic black women account for 30 percent of abortions. Hispanic women 25 percent, and women of other nonwhite races 9 percent. Of women obtaining abortions, 42 percent have incomes below 100 percent of the federal poverty level—$10,830 for a single woman with no children. http://www.guttmacher.org/pubs/fb_induced_abortion.html. *The Sacredness of Human Life*, 359.

35. Ibid.

INSANITY!

Although the reversal of abortion-on-demand rights, or at least (initially) the passing of legislation that would otherwise sharply restrict abortion is the hope of most believers, this hope would however, fail to address the problem of despair.[36] In fact, despair associated with abortion is an *intentional* cultural by-product in our nation.

David Gushee explains: "It is not too much to say that a society culturally constructed in the way ours now is actually *depends* on abortion to sustain its way of life. And women—especially poor women—are the ones who must endure the abortions that underwrite our social dysfunctionality."[37]

If a person's worldview—the controlling narrative by which they live their lives—does not include the *actual* historical event of the fall of man (Genesis 3) but rather they are a *progressive* or they are accepting of progressive policies on some level (that is, policies that "underwrite our social dysfunctionality"), how easy would it be for them to believe that pro-life advocates in general, and Christians in-particular are unsympathetic or uncaring regarding their "tragic desperation"? It is, perhaps, needless-to-say that the political left's progressive narrative exploits this vulnerability among the poor by boldly declaring the pro-life movement's "war on women."

This confronts the Christian with the scriptural mandate for us to live in obedience to Jesus' sermon: *"Settle matters quickly with your adversary . . ."* or in Paul's terms: *"If it is possible, as far as it depends on you, live at peace with everyone."* In our intensely politically charged culture, we need to create means for the "de-politicizing" of the Christian view regarding the sacredness of human life for the sake of civil dialogue and understanding.

Spiritual Formation

1. Please give your impression of the thesis statement: *Our vague notions of what it means to be human underlie absolutely every issue—religious, philosophical, political, racial, economical and the rule of law—in America today.*

2. *Have you personally ever been condemned for not "celebrating" abortion-on demand?*

---

36. Ibid.
37. Ibid., 359-360.

3. *If you knew a woman deeply distressed over whether to have an abortion or keep her baby, how would you begin a conversation about abortion with her?*

4. *What is your understanding of living life "by way of the Cross" as it specifically relates to this chapter, "Murder—The Sacredness of Life"?*

5. *How do you relate to others, especially those who are not like you?*

Chapter 4

"Do Not Commit Adultery"

Matthew 5:27-30

THE COMMUNAL NATURE OF *the Divine Image is uniquely revealed through the holy and honorable covenant of marriage.*

Jesus now turns from the sixth commandment—"You shall not murder," to the seventh—"You shall not commit adultery"

> **Matthew 5**—²⁷*"You have heard that it was said, 'You shall not commit adultery.'* ²⁸ *But I tell you that anyone who looks at a woman lustfully has already committed adultery with her in his heart.* ²⁹ *If your right eye causes you to stumble, gouge it out and throw it away. It is better for you to lose one part of your body than for your whole body to be thrown into hell.* ³⁰ *And if your right hand causes you to stumble, cut it off and throw it away. It is better for you to lose one part of your body than for your whole body to go into hell."*

Sexual Identities?

Contemporary confusion regarding sexual identity strains attempts to define sexual deviancy, especially, infidelity. For example, the progressive, politically correct, University of California system offers students six "gender identity" options on college admissions applications: "male; female; trans male/trans man; trans female/trans woman; gender queer/gender nonconforming; and different identity."[1]

---

1. Kohlhepp, "California Students Now Given Six 'Gender Identity' Choices."

"Do Not Commit Adultery"

How do we relate Christian understanding to contemporary views of sexuality and sexual identity?

To begin, what is a "progressive"? A secular progressive believes that their place in history is the ultimate, climatic point in human history: All that can be known, is now known. Progressive secularists are therefore historical skeptics—*Human thought is evolving and therefore, yesterday's knowledge is now obsolete. In a changing world, we need to assign new meanings to old ideas.*

Progressive secularism is the mold for the forming of the "fact/value dichotomy." The fact/value dichotomy has been recognized as foundational in the secular university since the 1920s. The fact/value dichotomy holds that we are not able to derive a value from a fact. In plain terms, "Since history cannot be relied upon to teach me anything about today, I need to interpret facts in-light of contemporary, evolving social norms and values." Therefore, the separation of facts and their interpretation is "a given"—an unspoken assumption—in the thinking of the secular progressive.[2]

Contemporary politics is rife with examples of the progressive fact/value dichotomy (i.e., the separation of facts and their interpretation). For example, the Obama Administration called on public school districts nationwide to allow transgender students to use the bathroom that matches their individual gender identity, regardless of their biological sex.

Guidelines for schools and transgender bathroom or locker room access that accords with their chosen sexual identity, rather than their biological sex, are outlined in: "U.S. Departments of Justice and Education Release Joint Guidance to Help Schools Ensure the Rights of Transgender Students."[3] Within the guidelines, former Attorney General of the United States, Loretta E. Lynch asserted: "There is no room in our schools for discrimination of any kind, including discrimination against transgender students on the basis of their sex."[4]

Therefore, when a transgender student informs their school of their chosen sexual identity, the school must treat the student consistent with the student's gender identity. The school may not require transgender students

---

2. Regrettably, the fact/value dichotomy is assumed in the thinking of a significant number of contemporary believers. The consequence of this is the "privatization" of believers' faith; that is, interpreting and applying it to the personal and spiritual realm only. "That way faith loses its *integrity* and becomes 'privately engaging and publicly irrelevant,'" Guinness, *The Case for Civility*, 100.

3. Department of Justice, Office of Public Affairs.

4. Ibid., page 1 of 3.

INSANITY!

to provide a medical diagnosis, undergo any medical treatment, or produce a birth certificate or other identification before treating them in a manner consistent with their gender identity.[5]

How is the fact/value dichotomy present in this example? In an article entitled: "How the Bathroom Became a Political Battleground for Civil Rights," *Washington Post* reporter, Monica Hess, observed that "Bathroom politics" are, "about the collision of those public spaces with cultural expectations at specific moments in time."[6] Hess (as well as progressives in general) ostensibly interprets the "bathroom politics" controversy in view of contemporary societal norms, that is, "specific moments in time."

Hess is therefore stating that, "*To me,* . . . bathroom politics are about the collision of those public spaces with cultural expectations at specific moments in time." The fact/value dichotomy equates *reality* with an individual's personal perspective, that is, "reality" directly corresponds with "the way I see it in this specific moment"—"It is, what it is."

Grounding sexual identities in subjective interpretation rather than objective reality presupposes the disappearance of the sacred [our "humanness" as related to our special creation]; and the loss of transcendence [faith—that is, our acknowledgment of God as basis for human dignity] and consequently, ethics are reduced to amoral politically correct categories.[7]

Progressives have cut themselves off from a transcendent moral-ethical Source and consequently, the faith, the ideas, the ethics and the way of life that form the foundation of the self-evident truths described in the Constitution, the Bill of Rights and the Declaration of Independence. Progressives have chosen to place themselves in a very vulnerable position—*Unless something is not evolving, that is, unless something is ultimately "fixed" or unchanging, how do you know how far something has evolved? How do you know if it's evolving instead of devolving?*

---

5. Ibid., page 2 of 3.

6. Hess, "How The Bathroom Became a Political Battleground for Civil Rights," page 3 of 10.

7. A significant portion of our culture view "morals" and "ethics" as synonyms. But they are not synonyms. Morals relate to "is-ness," that is, morals *describe* how humans behave. Ethics relate to "oughtness" that is, ethics inform us how humans *ought* to behave. When morals and ethics are confused by supposing they are synonyms, people conclude: "The way things *are* [morals] is the way they *ought* [ethics] to be." Therefore, whatever a person desires; and regardless of how they behave, they *ought* to be served and their behavior must be *tolerated* (accepted) by all.

"Do Not Commit Adultery"
Sex And The Marriage Covenant

Bonhoeffer echoes Paul's sexual ethics by stressing that, "Adherence to Jesus allows no free rein to desire unless it be accompanied by love."[8] Paul's instructions to the Thessalonians concerning sexual self-control, particularly adultery, are "in the Lord Jesus" (4:1), literally, "through" the Lord Jesus, and therefore, authoritative as the word of God for every age.

Paul is writing from Corinth to Thessalonica, two cities known for their unchecked immorality although, as Stott observes, not necessarily "any worse than other cities of that period in which it was widely accepted that men either could not or would not limit themselves to their wife as their only sexual partner."[9]

In verses 3-4, Paul writes: *³ "It is God's will that you should be sanctified: that you should avoid sexual immorality; ⁴ that each of you should learn to control your own body in a way that is holy and honorable. . .."* Paul says that it is God's will the Thessalonians "should be sanctified" or holy (the Greek term translated "sanctified" may refer to a process but more often, its result—"the state of being made holy").[10] Paul's imperative is for the Thessalonians to "avoid sexual immorality" (The Greek term *porneia*, translated, "sexual immorality," refers to "every kind of unlawful sexual intercourse."[11]).

In verse 4, Paul sets-forth two practical ethical principles: (1) Heterosexual marriage is the only context acceptable in God's sight for sexual intercourse; and (2) sexual relations, in the context of marriage, are to be "holy and honorable."[12]

The first half of verse 4 is difficult to understand; the literal translation is: *". . . each one of you should learn to control his own vessel in sanctification and honor."* The Greek term translated "vessel" is either a metaphor for "wife" or for "body."[13] Is Paul telling the Thessalonians to each take a wife or is he telling them to each control their own body?

---

8. Bonhoeffer, *The Cost of Discipleship*, 131.
9. Ibid., 81.
10. BAGD, 9.
11. Ibid., 693.
12. Stott, *The Gospel & The End of Time*, 82.
13. Ibid., 83.

INSANITY!

The verb "to control" normally means "to acquire" so it cannot be applied to one's body because we already have a body.[14] And, the Septuagint (*re:* The Septuagint, from around 225 B.C., is the Greek translation of the Old Testament Hebrew scriptures) uses Paul's term to mean "acquiring a wife."[15]

Since Paul is most likely referring to "acquiring a wife," the Apostle is affirming that heterosexual marriage is the only God-given context for sexual intercourse.[16] And sexual relations between husband and wife are to be "holy and honorable," sexual desire in the context of marriage is to be "accompanied by love."

Therefore, sex in the context of the marriage covenant is to be purged of any "dishonorable associations."[17] Verse 4 literally begins with "To know" (Greek, *eidenai*) and so, rather than the NIV rendering, "each of you should learn. . ." a better understanding is, each one "should respect his wife;" "honorable" is used by Paul to contrast with ". . . *passionate lust like the heathen, who do not know God*" (verse 5).

"Adherence to Jesus allows no free rein to desire . . ." (Bonhoeffer) and therefore, "in this matter no one should 'overstep' ("transgress, break laws and commandments,"[18]) or "wrong" ("take advantage of, outwit, defraud, or cheat"[19]) his [wife] or take advantage of [her]" (verse 6).[20]

In marriage, man and woman are made one flesh as husband and wife: "*For this reason a man will leave his father and mother and be united to his wife, and they will become one flesh*" (Gen. 2:24). And thus, the covenant of marriage is, "a two-person union unlike any other in its importance to the committed individuals"[21]: *The communal nature of the Divine Image is uniquely revealed through the holy covenant of marriage.*

---

14. BAGD, 455.
15. Stott, *The Gospel & The End of Time*, 83.
16. Ibid.
17. Ibid., 84.
18. BAGD, 840.
19. Ibid., 667.
20. My brackets for "wife" and "her" follows from the better rendering, "should respect his wife."
21. *The Catholic World Report*, "Excerpts from 'Obergefell v. Hodges,'" 2 of 4.

"Do Not Commit Adultery"
Living In The Way Of Jesus

The Pharisees were content to simply avoid the act of adultery as means to pleasing God. But the Pharisees' too narrow definition of sexual immorality allowed for too broad of a definition of sexual purity. Jesus then countered the error of the Pharisees by affirming a much wider understanding of God's commandment to not commit adultery. Matthew 5: [27]*"You have heard that it was said, 'You shall not commit adultery.'* [28] *But I tell you that anyone who looks at a woman lustfully has already committed adultery with her in his heart."* "As the prohibition of murder included the angry thought and the insulting word," observes Stott, "so the prohibition of adultery included the lustful look and imagination."[22]

How can we maintain sexual purity in a sex-crazed, wildly perverse and permissive cultural environment like modern-day America? Jesus' wisdom leads us to an understanding of the relation between the eyes and the heart for practical resolve of our vulnerability to lust. Matthew 5: [29] *If your right eye causes you to stumble, gouge it out and throw it away. It is better for you to lose one part of your body than for your whole body to be thrown into hell.* [30] *And if your right hand causes you to stumble, cut it off and throw it away. It is better for you to lose one part of your body than for your whole body to go into hell."*

If the lust of the eyes leads to adultery in the heart, then the controlling of the eyes will lead to the controlling of a vulnerable, lustful heart. Jesus' anti-dote for a lustful eye is to *"gouge it out and throw it away."* Tragically, there have been some whose zeal far exceeded their wisdom, and they took Jesus literally. For example, Democritus determined to overcome lust by blinding himself.[23] And Origen, a third-century theologian, whose ascetic practices were often to the extreme, applied a too-literal interpretation to Matthew 19:12: *"For some are eunuchs because they were born that way; and others were made that way by men; and others have renounced marriage because of the kingdom of heaven. The one who can accept this should accept it."* Origen's literal "acceptance" resulted in his making himself a eunuch.[24]

Jesus is not recommending literal physical maiming but rather, moral self-denial; "Not mutilation but mortification is the path to holiness he

---

22. Stott, *The Message of the Sermon on the Mount*, 87.

23. Tertullian, *Apology*, 46.11-12. In: Keener, *Matthew*, 117.

24. In 325 A.D the Council of Nicaea rejected such barbarous practices among Christians.

taught, and 'mortification' or 'taking up the cross' to follow Christ means to reject sinful practices so resolutely that we die to them or put them to death."[25] If our eye is the origin of our temptation, that is, a woman (or man) we see, then the spiritual application of gouging out our eye is simply, don't look! "Behave," says Stott, "as if you had actually plucked out your eyes and flung them away, were now blind and so *could not* see the objects which previously caused you to sin."[26] And likewise, if either your hand or foot causes you to sin because of what you do or where you go, then sever them; that is, don't do whatever or go wherever you are vulnerable to temptation and sin.

Obedience to the commandment: *"Love your neighbor as yourself"* requires "... giving and receiving genuine Christian love with the appropriate boundaries—dealing with people as human beings [image bearers] like ourselves rather than objects of our passion is an important defense against lust."[27]

Spiritual Formation

1. What is the primary theme of this chapter?
2. What are some implications of our special creation and human sexuality?
3. What is the fact/value dichotomy? How does it influence a person's ethical point of view?
4. If humanity were evolved instead of created, how would human sexuality be distinguished?
5. How do we relate the Christian ethic to contemporary views of sexual identities? How does this influence your relationships with LGBTQ people?

---

25. Stott, *The Message of the Sermon on the Mount*, 89.
26. Ibid.
27. Keener, *Matthew*, 119.

Chapter 5

Marriage and Divorce

Matthew 5:31-32

MARRIAGE IS A SACRED *union, a covenant relationship, in which the Divine Image is uniquely revealed.*

> **Mt. 5—**³¹ *"It has been said, 'Anyone who divorces his wife must give her a certificate of divorce.'* ³² *But I tell you that anyone who divorces his wife, except for sexual immorality, makes her the victim of adultery, and anyone who marries a divorced woman commits adultery.*

Same-Sex Marriage And The Created Order

Reflecting on the nature of God and His creation, James DeYoung observes: "The only model of sexual expression contemplated in Scripture is that which is patterned after the creation model of Genesis 1-2."[1] The creation narratives, continues De Young, ". . . point to the communal nature of the divine image. Implicit in the first creation narrative but more explicit in the second is the idea that God makes the first human pair so that humans may enjoy community with each other."[2]

God is the foundation for our existence: ²⁷*"So God created mankind in his own image, in the image of God he created them; male and female he created them."* Adam was aware of his "solitude;" his sense of incompleteness was sexual in nature and therefore, when he was blessed with his sexual counterpart, his joy overflowed. She is "bone of my bones and flesh of my

---

1. DeYoung, "The Meaning of 'Nature' in Romans 1 And Its Implications," 440.
2. Grenz, "Theological Foundations for Male-Female Relationships," 621.

INSANITY!

flesh" (Gen. 2:23). Contrary to the narcissistic inclination of "sameness," when "we are confronted with the other who is sexually different from us we are reminded of our own incompleteness."[3]

On June 26, 2015, the Supreme Court of the United States ruled that individual states can no longer ban same-sex marriage. By a 5-4[4] ruling, the Supreme Court established same-sex marriage a civil right in America.

Justice Kennedy stressed that the advocates for same-sex marriage (the petitioners) seek the liberty to marry someone of the same sex; and that their marriages would be recognized lawful on the same terms and conditions as marriages between persons of the opposite sex.[5]

Moreover, Justice Kennedy asserted that under the Due Process Clause of the Fourteenth Amendment, no State shall "deprive any person of life, liberty, or property, without due process of law."[6] These liberties, Kennedy insisted, are extended "to certain personal choices central to individual dignity and autonomy," to include "intimate choices that define personal identity and beliefs . . . ."[7]

Justice Kennedy further opined that it is, "clear that the challenged laws burden the liberty of same-sex couples, and it must be additionally acknowledged that they abridge central precepts of equality .. . . The imposition of this disability on gays and lesbians serves to disrespect and subordinate them."[8]

Is the limiting of marriage to one man and one woman by those who oppose same-sex marriage—e.g., evangelical Christians—intended to demean gay people?

Romans 1:18-32—"Due Penalty"

Paul's intent in Romans 1:18-32 is to describe how idolatry is a primary cause of cultural collapse (*et. al.*, Chapter 1, Lawlessness and the Created

---

3. Ibid.

4. Chief Justice John Roberts, along with Justice Clarence Thomas, Justice Samuel Alito and Justice Antonin Scalia dissented. Justice Anthony Kennedy voted with the four liberal justices to affirm same-sex marriage is now a civil right.

5. The Catholic Report, "Essential Excerpts from 'Obergefell v. Hodges,' Majority Opinion."

6. Ibid.

7. Ibid.

8. Ibid., 2.

Order). Paul's reference to the Creator and His creation would not have escaped the understanding of his Jewish-Christian audience, not only regarding the created order but also the natural teleology (design) of male and female within the created order.

Paul's argument in Romans 1 is founded on the nature of God's creation.[9] The Apostle is asserting that homosexuality is a transgression of God's natural teleology (design) for His creation. And [26] *"Because of this, God gave them over to shameful lusts. Even their women exchanged natural sexual relations for unnatural ones.* [27] *In the same way the men also abandoned natural relations with women and were inflamed with lust for one another. Men committed shameful acts with other men and received in themselves the due penalty for their error,"* Rom. 1:26-27.

Paul speaks of "natural" and "unnatural" behavior in verse 26; and "natural relations" in verse 27. Some have attempted to argue that the Apostle's reference here to "nature" (*physis*) means, "what is natural to me."[10] The argument following this contention is that Paul is not referring to those whose nature (or orientation) is homosexual; rather he is condemning heterosexuals who are acting as homosexuals and perverting the true nature of those who, by nature, are homosexuals.

Another related understanding of "nature," as used by Paul, is that this concept is derived from Greek, rather than Jewish sources.[11] Paul, then, is condemning pederasty (sodomy between a man and a boy), instead of mutual adult-adult homosexuality.[12]

Now, whereas *physis*, meaning nature, is common in secular Greek, there is absolutely no indication that it means "what is natural to me."[13] And neither is there any indication that *physis* (nature) is used by Paul to refer to pederasty. Such arguments are founded on the erroneous notion that Greco-Roman culture was the source for New Testament assertions regarding homosexuality.

---

9. Kittel and Friedrich, *Theological Dictionary of the New Testament*, Vol. IX, 273. At the time Paul wrote his letters to the primitive churches, there was no word in classical, biblical, or patristic Greek which corresponded with our English term "homosexual." Instead, homosexual behavior was described in graphic terms. Virtually all Greek lexicons, including standard English lexicons, conclude that homoeroticism is in view.

10. Boswell, *Christianity, Social Tolerance and Homosexuality,* 107-117. And Scanzoni and Mollenkott, *Is the Homosexual My Neighbor?* 61-68.

11. Bailey, *Homosexuality and the Western Christian Tradition*, 38.

12. Scroggs, *The New Testament and Homosexuality*, 116-117.

13. BAGD, 869-870.

INSANITY!

The Apostle's references to Creator and creation (1:19-23) frame his argument against homosexuality in 1:26-27. Plato and the Greeks had no transcendent Creator; they deified nature and therefore saw "natural" very differently from Paul. Paul's worldview is unequivocally Jewish. Additionally, Paul's language supports the idea of homosexuality involving adult-adult mutuality, "Paul writes literally 'males with males committing indecent acts'; he does not say 'men with boys' (as Plato is capable of saying: *Laws* 836a-c)."[14]

Further, Paul compares lesbianism with male homosexuality, "As lesbianism was usually between adults in mutuality, so the force of the comparative argues for male adult-adult mutuality."[15] And finally, "shameful lusts" (v.26); "inflamed with lust for one another" and "in themselves" (v.27) support both the argument that Paul's moral understanding is thoroughly Jewish and that adult sexual relations are intended by the Apostle.

In Romans 1:26, Paul speaks of, *"nature as the regular natural order."* [16] God's judgment, because of the perversion of the *natural* order ("natural" appears twice; and "unnatural" appears once in verses 26-27), is "penal recompense" (KJV) or "the due penalty" (NIV). That is, *"In R. 1:27 the unnatural sexual aberration of men is regarded as a punishment for the fact that they do not pay God the honor which is His due. Where men worship idols instead of God, the destruction of human society is the evident consequence* (1:28ff.)."[17] If God's punishment for homoerotic behavior is for the person to be bound by that very behavior, then Romans 1:27 supports the notion that people are *not* born gay.

Although the origins of homosexual behavior are varied, the biblical evidence is that homosexual behavior is acquired instead of biological. God's judgment, "penal recompense" or "the due penalty," is just. However, as revealed in 1 Corinthians 6:9-11, God's grace is all surpassing—*"And that is what some of you were. But you were washed, you were sanctified, you were justified in the name of the Lord Jesus Christ and by the Spirit of our God."*

---

14. DeYoung, "The Meaning of 'Nature' in Romans 1," 439.

15. Ibid.

16. BAGD, 869.

17. Kittel and Friedrich, *Theological Dictionary of the New Testament*, Vol. IV, 702. (Italics, final sentence of the quote, are mine for purpose of emphasizing the theme of the book).

Marriage and Divorce

1 Corinthians 6:9-11—"Once You Were, But Now You Are Not"!

In 1 Cor. 6:9-10, Paul writes: *⁹ "Do you not know that the wicked will not inherit the kingdom of God? Do not be deceived: Neither the sexually immoral nor idolaters nor adulterers nor male prostitutes nor homosexual offenders ¹⁰ nor thieves nor the greedy nor drunkards nor slanderers nor swindlers will inherit the kingdom of God."*

The word translated, "wicked" (Grk: *adikoi*) (6:9) is the same word translated "ungodly" (*adikon*) in 6:1. Neither the ungodly (6:1) or the wicked (6:9) will inherit the kingdom of God. Paul appears to be warning "the saints" that if they continue to behave like "the wicked," they will not inherit the kingdom of God.

In 5:9, Paul reminds the Corinthians that he has written them to inform them not to associate with "sexually immoral people."[18] But please note, Paul informs the Corinthians that he is *". . . not at all meaning the people of this world who are immoral . . . . In that case you would have to leave this world. But now I am writing you that you must not associate with anyone who calls himself a brother but is sexually immoral . . . . With such a man do not even eat"* (5:9-11).[19]

In 6:9, Paul refers to: *". . . the sexually immoral nor idolaters nor adulterers nor male prostitutes nor homosexual offenders . . . ."* The Greek terms translated, "male prostitutes" (*malakoi*) and "homosexual offenders" (*arsenokoitai*) require thorough explanation.

Gordon Fee observes: "The first word, *malakoi* ("male prostitutes") has the basic meaning of 'soft'; but it also became a pejorative epithet for men who were 'soft' or 'effeminate,' most likely referring to the younger, 'passive' partner in pederasty,[20] the most common form of homosexuality in the Greco-Roman world."[21]

In the Greco-Roman world, effeminate young men prostituted themselves to older men. However, the term *malakoi* was seldom used to

---

18. Re: "sexually immoral," Paul is referring to a:*"fornicator, one who practices sexual immorality,"* BAGD, 693.

19. In his letter to the Corinthians, Paul is addressing a significant degree of immorality: in 6:12-20, the subject matter is sexual immorality and in 8:1-11:1, the subject matter is idolatry.

20. Louw & Nida, *Greek-English Lexicon of the New Testament*, Vol. 1, 79.100 and 88.281.

21. Fee, *The First Epistle to the Corinthians*, 243.

INSANITY!

describe "male prostitutes," nevertheless, in this context, the term appears to be describing this form of behavior.[22]

Slightly distinguished from "male prostitutes" are "homosexual offenders." The Greek term *arsenokoitai* appears to refer to male homosexuality, particularly the "active" partner.[23] The seeming association between the two terms, *malakoi* and *arsenokoitai*, serves to substantiate the former as referring to "male prostitutes."[24]

The Greek word translated, "homosexual offenders" (*aresenokoitai*) is a compound term: "male" (*areseno*) and "intercourse" (*koitai*).[25] Together, these two terms are included in a list of vices, mostly sexual sins. Fee therefore, concludes: "Although one cannot be certain, it is very likely that the NIV is moving toward a proper understanding by translating 'male prostitute' and 'homosexual offender,' with the proviso that 'male prostitute' most likely denotes a consenting homosexual youth."[26]

Paul concludes verse 10 with the warning he began verse 9 with, viz., "the wicked" (those guilty of every vice in his list) will not "*. . . inherit the kingdom of God.*"

But Paul does not conclude his fuller argument with condemnation, rather he points to the finished work of Christ in verse 11: *"And that is what some of you were. But you were washed, you were sanctified, you were justified in the name of the Lord Jesus Christ and by the Spirit of our God."*

Paul distinguishes the Corinthian Church from the wicked, who persist in sexual immorality, idolatry, male prostitution, homoeroticism, thievery, greed, drunkenness, slandering, and swindling—"And that is what some of you were"—*but* you no longer are because you have been baptized into Christ ("washed"[27])—*but* you have been set apart unto Christ ("sanctified")—*but* your "faith is credited as righteousness" ("justified") *". . . in the name of the Lord Jesus Christ and by the Spirit of our God."*

In the Greek sentence, the three verbs, "washed," "sanctified," and "justified," are preceded by the adversative, "but." The adversative [but]

---

22. Ibid., 244.

23. Louw & Nida, *Greek-English Lexicon of the New Testament*, 88.280.

24. Fee, *The First Epistle to the Corinthians*, 244.

25. The term, *koitai* is vulgar slang for "intercourse" and this may be, according to Fee, why this term is seldom found in the literature, Ibid.

26. Ibid. Fee concludes his thoughts, *re:* 6:9-10: "For Paul's attitude toward homosexuality in general one need refer only to his own Jewish background with its abhorrence of such, plus his description of such activity" (Rom. 1:26-27).

27. BAGD, 96.

"... gives additional force to the 'once you were' but 'now you are not.'" [28] The inherent imperative here calls the Corinthians to "... live out this new life in Christ and stop being like the wicked."[29]

The adversative ["but"] strongly implies that just as some were formerly thieves, drunkards and swindlers, likewise, those who were formerly engaged in homoerotic behavior ("homosexual offenders"), are now through faith in the finished work of Christ, no longer subject to "... *the due penalty for their perversion*" (*cf.* Rom. 1:27)

Is the limiting of marriage to one man and one woman by those who oppose same-sex marriage—e.g., evangelical Christians—intended to demean gay people?

In a word, "No." To the contrary, why would anyone, but especially a believer, encourage a person—an image bearer of God—to persist in "the due penalty for their perversion" instead of repenting and turning to Christ and experiencing the indescribable joy of being "washed," and "sanctified," and "justified" in "the name of the Lord Jesus Christ and by the Spirit of our God"?

And further, human dignity is founded on our distinctively "male and female" special creation in the image of God. This ancient distinction—the communal nature of the Divine Image—is uniquely revealed in the holy covenant of marriage. It then follows that advocacy for same-sex marriage profoundly demeans the personal dignity of gay men and women. Shame on the Supreme Court of the United States of America.

Jesus' timeless wisdom concerning the sacredness of marriage and the need to place a hedge around its God ordained intentions now follows.

'Haven't You Read. . .?'

John Stott appropriately assumes that Matthew 5:31-32 is "an abbreviated summary" of Jesus' teaching on marriage and divorce.[30] A fuller context of Jesus' view of divorce is found in Matthew 19:3-9: *³ Some Pharisees came to him to test him. They asked, "Is it lawful for a man to divorce his wife for any and every reason?" ⁴ "Haven't you read," he replied, "that at the beginning the Creator 'made them male and female,' ⁵ and said, 'For this reason a man will leave his father and mother and be united to his wife, and the two will*

---

28. Fee, *The First Epistle to the Corinthians*, 245.

29. Ibid.

30. Stott, *The Message of the Sermon on the Mount*, 92-93.

INSANITY!

become one flesh'? ⁶ *So they are no longer two, but one flesh. Therefore, what God has joined together, let no one separate."* ⁷ *"Why then,"* they asked, *"did Moses command that a man give his wife a certificate of divorce and send her away?"* ⁸ *Jesus replied, "Moses permitted you to divorce your wives because your hearts were hard. But it was not this way from the beginning.* ⁹ *I tell you that anyone who divorces his wife, except for sexual immorality, and marries another woman commits adultery."*

Although the pharisaic parties of Hillel and Shammai were fierce rivals, they were united in their efforts to force Jesus into taking sides in an ongoing debate concerning the legal and moral implications of divorce. Typical of the Pharisees, both rabbinic schools were more concerned with what was *permissible*—*"Can a man "divorce his wife for any and every reason?"*—than with what is righteous under God's sovereign reign.

Since the Pharisees believed, Moses "commanded" a man seeking to divorce his wife to give her *"a certificate of divorce and send her away,"* neither rabbinic school ever considered what was righteous (or unrighteous) concerning the breaking of the sacred covenant of marriage. What was "a certificate of divorce" and why did Moses, in the understanding of the Pharisees, prescribe it in the law?

In the law, specifically, Deuteronomy 24:1-4, the "certificate of divorce" is introduced as an instrument for the dissolving of a marriage.[31] However, Moses did not "prescribe" the certificate of divorce *per se*, as presumed by the Pharisees. Rather Moses is merely acknowledging divorce as a cultural practice[32]: *"If a man marries a woman who becomes displeasing to him because he finds something indecent about her, and he writes her a certificate of divorce, gives it to her and sends her from his house,* ² *and if after she leaves his house she becomes the wife of another man,* ³ *and her second husband dislikes her and writes her a certificate of divorce, gives it to her and sends her from his house, or if he dies,* ⁴ *then her first husband, who divorced her, is not allowed to marry her again after she has been defiled. That would*

---

31. Keener notes that the Biblical imagery in Deuteronomy 24:1-4 (and elsewhere in Scripture, e.g., Dt. 22:13-21; 22:28-29; Lev. 21:7, 14; Is. 50:1, Mt. 5:31-32,19:3-9), addresses the woman because in the patriarchal Palestinian culture, men were permitted to marry more than one wife, but sharing a wife was considered adultery. *Matthew*, Osborne, Briscoe and Robinson,119-120.

32. The reader will observe how the passage, Deuteronomy 24:1-4, is written in the form of a supposed scenario.

be detestable in the eyes of the Lord. Do not bring sin upon the land the Lord your God is giving you as an inheritance (Dt. 24:1-4).[33]

The "certificate of divorce" reference applies to a woman who is divorced by her first husband because he finds "something indecent about her." The Hebrew term (*erwath dabar*) used here literally means: "nakedness of a thing."[34] Although it is unclear what "something indecent" or "nakedness of a thing" precisely refers to, in the thinking of the Shammaite wing of the Pharisees, it referred to "some form of inappropriate sexual behavior."[35]

Rabbi Shammai's conservative school appears to have followed this understanding, teaching that divorce was permitted only for some "grave matrimonial offense, something evidently 'unseemly' or 'indecent'"[36] but, nevertheless, "behavior short of adultery, which was officially punishable by death."[37]

Rabbi Hillel's liberal school argued for a broad interpretation of "something indecent" to include a variety of the wife's offenses, e.g., she burnt her husband's food, she was disobedient or perhaps her husband became attracted to a more beautiful woman,[38] that is, *"for any and every reason."* Rabbi Hillel's interpretation appears to be the prevailing opinion (*cf.*19:3). But whose side is Jesus on in this legal-moral debate, the legalists or the liberals, the Shammaites or the Hillelites?

Jesus is on neither side, instead he reframes the marriage and divorce debate among the Pharisees beginning with three words: "Haven't you read . . . .?" (19:4a). These are the teachers of the Law but because they are so involved with seeking ways that permit themselves to do less, the Pharisees have missed the whole point of what Moses had intended!

In keeping with many other Old Testament laws intended to "place a hedge" of protection around the vulnerable, the primary purpose of Moses' instruction in Deuteronomy was to provide some legal relief for women living in a profoundly patriarchal society. In other words, "the certificate of

---

33. Ancient Israel employed the certificate of divorce based on the assumption that once the husband served his wife with the certificate, she was free to remarry. However, and this is the issue in Deuteronomy 24:1-4, she is not free to remarry her first husband (v. 4).

34. Stassen & Gushee, *Kingdom Ethics*, 279.

35. Ibid.

36. Stott, *The Message of the Sermon on the Mount*, 92.

37. Stassen & Gushee, *Kingdom Ethics*, 279.

38. Ibid.

divorce" that was originally "intended to protect women from being casually divorced was now being examined in search of commands and permissions enabling men to know when they might initiate divorce."³⁹

Jesus undercuts the pharisaic debate and draws the rival parties back to creation and God's original intention for marriage: ⁴ *"Haven't you read . . ., that at the beginning the Creator made them male and female,' ⁵ and said, 'For this reason a man will leave his father and mother and be united to his wife, and the two will become one flesh'? ⁶ So they are no longer two, but one flesh. Therefore, what God has joined together let no one separate"* (Mt. 19:4-6).

Jesus points to marriage as a sacred union between two people, male and female. This sacred union is a covenant relationship and as one flesh, the Divine Image is uniquely revealed in them. Therefore, do God's will, seek to reconcile with your wife instead of asking permission to do less.⁴⁰

Matthew 5:32 (*cf.* Mt. 19:9) refers to an exception clause regarding divorce:

> ³²*"But I tell you that anyone who divorces his wife, except for sexual immorality, makes her the victim of adultery, and anyone who marries a divorced woman commits adultery."*

The Greek term translated "sexual immorality" (*porneia*) has been translated "adultery" (NIV). Therefore, many believers have concluded that Jesus' teaching does not allow divorce except in the case of adultery; but when that happens, remarriage is permissible. However, in a Jewish context, this understanding would place Jesus on the side of the Shammaites. Nevertheless, many churches today embrace this view.

But, of course, since adultery was punishable by death in an ancient Jewish context, it is very unlikely that adultery is inferred in Matthew 5:32 or 19:9. Other translations (e.g., KJV, "fornication," NASB, "unchastity," Philipps, "unfaithfulness") appear to support the notion that the word "nakedness" (*"erwa"*) is used often as an idiom for sexual intercourse, therefore, sexual connotations are most likely intended in Jesus' debate with the Shammaites and the Hillelites.⁴¹

---

39. Ibid.

40. My commentary is a partial paraphrase of Stassen & Gushee who say, "Jesus was saying to his followers: do God's will for marriage and stop asking when it is permissible to do less," *Kingdom Ethics*, 277.

41. Spinkle, "Sexuality, Sexual Ethics," *Dictionary of the Old Testament: Pentateuch*, Alexander and Baker, 744. In: Stott, *A Deeper Look at the Sermon on the Mount*, 76.

Further, as above mentioned, Matthew uses a term (Greek, *porneia*) generally used for sexual sin in a broad sense (e.g., premarital intercourse; and other forms of "unchastity," or "sexual immorality") *rather* than the Greek word (*moicheia*) specifically used for adultery.[42]

The variety of translations infer an apparent awareness of the Palestinian cultural context. And to include the confusion generated by the Pharisees and as well as the use of the word *porneia* ("sexual immorality") instead of *moicheia* ("adultery") indicates that Jesus intended to say, contrary to the Shammaites more narrow view, that divorce may be "permitted" (not "commanded") as a morally acceptable option in cases other than adultery. That is, whenever a spouse behaves indecently or unchastely in terms of patterned (unrepentant) behavior. And, also, this conclusion is very much contrary to the too-broad Hillelite point of view that divorce is "commanded" for *"any and every reason."*

Living In The Way Of Jesus

In his first letter to the Corinthians, Paul's counsel concerning divorce and remarriage for an ancient Greek church is timely for 21st Century Western Christians living with a "unique understanding of the time of the End."

Paul points to the Lord's commandment, 1 Cor. 7:10-11: [10] *"To the married I give this command (not I, but the Lord): A wife must not separate from her husband.* [11] *But if she does, she must remain unmarried or else be reconciled to her husband. And a husband must not divorce his wife."*

1 Corinthians 7 is divided into two sections: vv. 1-24 and vv. 25-40. In both sections, Paul addresses marital matters involving sexual relations, divorce, second marriages and marriage itself.[43] A "controlling motif" (Fee) in Paul's answers to the questions about marriage posed by the Corinthians is: "Do not seek a change in status"[44] (re: vv. 17-24).

Specifically, the context for 1 Corinthians 7:10-11 appears to call into question a movement developing among these ancient Christians that stressed the need to abstain from sexual relations for the sake of holiness. Women in the church were anticipating the need to divorce their husbands so that they could devote themselves to the Lord: "In particular, women in mixed marriages were considering divorce because they found it hard to

---

42. Stassen & Gushee, *Kingdom Ethics*, 285.
43. Fee, *The First Epistle to the Corinthians*, 267.
44. Ibid., 268.

reconcile sexual relations with an unbeliever and holy participation in the body of Christ (cf. 1 Cor. 6:12-20)."[45]

Paul's response to such "sexual asceticism" (Stassen & Gushee) stresses the need to not "seek a change in status," that is, continue in your "marital duty" towards one another (1 Cor. 7:2-6). But if the women do divorce their husbands, they must "remain unmarried or else be reconciled" to their husbands.

Paul asserts that this teaching is from "the Lord" and his focus is on the unfortunate but common condition of "relational brokenness and alienation" in marriage that sometimes results in an isolated act, "such as an impetuous affair."[46] More often, of course, serious martial problems are the result of layers of unresolved conflict and resentment accumulated over the course of years. But in every instance of marital discord, Paul stresses reconciliation and conformity to God's will for a husband and wife (1 Cor. 7: 12-16).[47]

Paul's emphasis, throughout 1 Corinthians 7, is *reconciliation*, either involving a misled spouse (vv. 1-7); an unbelieving spouse (vv. 12-16); personal inner-conflict (vv. 8-9; 18-24); and special relational circumstances (vv. 25-38). The Apostle stresses that "*. . . each one should retain the place in life that the Lord assigned to him and to which God has called him. This is the rule I [Paul] lay down in all the churches*" (v. 17). Paul calls on believers to shift their focus from themselves to a kingdom vision of marriage centered in the Cross and divine reconciliation.

But what if efforts to reconcile break-down? What if a husband divorces his wife, contrary to Paul's apostolic imperative (7: 10-11)?

Verses 10-11 set-forth the ideal, that is, marriage for a life-time. Paul, however, provides a permissive alternative, or an exception, in 1 Corinthians 7:15, "*But if the unbelieving partner separates, let it be so. A believing man or woman is not bound in such circumstances; God has called us to live*

---

45. Stassen & Gushee, *Kingdom Ethics*, 286.

46. Ibid., 287. Re: Reconciliation, Stassen & Gushee comment: "It is the end product of the cycle of peacemaking that Jesus teaches throughout the Sermon on the Mount: acknowledging that we are trapped in a vicious cycle, seeking to participate in God's gracious deliverance, taking the initiative to go to the other, *seeking reconciliation*, refusing to take vengeance, affirming the other's valid interests, repenting rather than judging, forgiving rather than withholding forgiveness, and praying for the adversary and , above all and in all, love."

47. Significant here is Paul's emphasis on the benefit for the unbeliever regards their sanctity instead of any loss for the believer, Ibid. 288.

in peace." Paul does not change what he received from the Lord as stated in 7:11b, but he qualifies it in 7:15, *desertion* is an exception to 7:11. Consequently, the deserted woman or man must not be denied the opportunity to remarry.

Further clarification regarding Paul's instructions is in order. The "But" (*de*) that Paul introduces his thought with, [11] *"But if she does..."* has the sense of "rather."[48] The "rather" transcends Paul's present discussion and points to a kingdom vision for life, *"God has called us to live in peace."* The phrase, *"is not bound"* (7:15b), is literally, "has not been enslaved," warrants a broadened application. Though not explicitly mentioned, spousal abuse, physically and psychologically, excessive perversion (pornography) and gross immorality in general, criminal behavior, substance abuse or child endangerment are all an abandonment of the marriage covenant.

Many, to include Luther, have concluded that 1 Corinthians 7:15 provides grounds for divorce and remarriage. But two things must be strongly reaffirmed: (1) Paul's "rule" for all the churches is *reconciliation;* but if reconciliation fails, (2) It is unclear if the abandoned spouse has a right to remarry *unless* the unbeliever marries first.[49]

Spiritual Formation

1. *How were the Pharisees, both the Shammaites and the Hillelites, misunderstanding Moses and divorce?*
2. *How was Jesus protecting wives in a profoundly patriarchal culture?*
3. *What are your impressions of Paul's exception to divorce and remarriage in 1Cor. 7:15? More specifically, what is your impression of my assertion that the phrase, "is not bound" (v.15) warrants a "broadened application": "Though not explicitly mentioned, spousal abuse, physically and psychologically, excessive perversion (pornography) and gross*

---

48. *Theological Dictionary of the New Testament*, Kittel, Vol. II, 416.

49. Robertson, *Word Pictures in the New Testament*, Volume VI, 128. Regarding "unbeliever" and the abandoning of the marriage covenant. In close to 30 years as a lead pastor, I have seen many cases where a Christian has abandoned another Christian. In these cases, I do not judge the one who abandons to be an "unbeliever," such a judgment belongs to God only. I do however acknowledge that the kind of behavior that accompanies "abandonment" is certainly non-Christian and subject to God's judgment.

INSANITY!

immorality in general, criminal behavior, substance abuse or child endangerment are all an abandonment of the marriage covenant"?

4. *Why would the believer not be free to remarry until the unbeliever is remarried?(Note, Paul appears to assume that the believer would not dissert the unbeliever).*

5. *This question should be answered in true [Biblical], Christian love: If two people love one another, shouldn't they be allowed to marry even if they are of the same sex?*

6. *How does Justice Kennedy's assertion: "The imposition of this disability on gay and lesbians serves to disrespect and subordinate them" actually end in demeaning gay and lesbian people?*

Chapter 6

Oaths

Matthew 5:33-37

IF A STATEMENT, CLAIM *or one's testimony is true, it must conform to God's character, that is, ultimate reality, as revealed in God's created order and/or special revelation, holy Scripture.*

> **Matthew 5—**[33] "Again, you have heard that it was said to the people long ago, 'Do not break your oath, but fulfill to the Lord the vows you have made.' [34] But I tell you, do not swear an oath at all: either by heaven, for it is God's throne; [35] or by the earth, for it is his footstool; or by Jerusalem, for it is the city of the Great King. [36] And do not swear by your head, for you cannot make even one hair white or black. [37] All you need to say is simply 'Yes' or 'No'; anything beyond this comes from the evil one.

What is an oath? Bonhoeffer affirms: "It is an appeal made to God in public, calling upon him to witness a statement made in connection with an event or fact, past, present or future."[1] Simply, an oath involves truth-telling.

We must not swear by anything in the created order, heaven or earth, "for it is his footstool." Heaven and earth are God's creation. Or by Jerusalem, "for it is the city of the Great King," the earthly Jerusalem is a mere symbol of the Jerusalem above "and God swears only by himself, that is,

---

1. Bonhoeffer, *The Cost of Discipleship*, 136.

INSANITY!

by his own glory;"[2] and neither "by your head," for this is self-worship.[3] We must not give to creation "the honor of divine veneration"[4] as pagans do (Romans 1: 21-23; 25). The law demands that no one swears falsely; but Jesus says, we must not "swear an oath at all."

"What Is Truth"?

The majority are empowered by their construction of abstract metanarratives or paradigms, e.g., Nazism, Stalinism, Fascism and Communism, that serve to marginalize the disenfranchised, the weak (minorities), the poor, and the vulnerable.

A "metanarrative is an overarching story that claims to contain truth applicable to all people at all times in all cultures."[5] The French term, *grand recits*, translated "metanarratives" literally means "big stories."[6] Postmodern is defined by its suspicion of big stories or abstract metanarratives.[7]

Instead of "big stories" (metanarratives), the narrative a progressive/ postmodern community creates for themselves is their own private "reality" or "truth."[8] *That is, in a progressive/postmodern context, "truth" is founded on what the narrative means to the community rather than what it really (actually) means.*

#Black Lives Matter: A Contemporary Example Of "Truth-Telling"

Outside the gates of the Minnesota State Fair Black Lives Matter protesters in St. Paul chanted: "Pigs in a blanket, fry 'em like bacon."[9] And in New

---

2. Cyril of Alexandria, "Fragmenta in Matthaeum," 63, In: *Ancient Christian Commentary on Scripture, Matthew 1-13*, Simonetti; Oden, 116.

3. Chrysostom, "The Gospel of Matthew," Homily,17.5-6, Ibid.

4. Chromatius, "Tractate on Matthew 24.3.I-4, Ibid.

5. Frost & Hirsch, *The Shaping of Things to Come, Innovation and Mission for the 21st – Century Church*, 8.

6. Smith, *Who's Afraid of Postmodernism?* 63.

7. Lyotard defines postmodern "as incredulity towards metanarratives," *The Postmodern Condition: A Report on Knowledge*, Vol. 10, xxiv.

8. For an academic treatment of post-modernity, please see my, *A Letter from Christ*, pages 13-23.

9. Ross, "Black Lives Protesters Chant: 'Pigs In A Blanket Fry 'Em Like Bacon."

York City, Black Lives Matter protesters shouted: "What do we want? Dead cops! When do we want it? Now!"[10]

Black Lives Matter is, to say the least, a controversial example of a progressive/postmodern movement or community. Although 84% of all adult Americans (87% of white and 82% of black) believe, "There is a lot of anger and hostility between the different ethnic and racial groups in America today," about half (52%) of the general population completely miss the point of this angry group's label: "Black lives matter."[11] They react to the notion, "Black Lives Matter," by exclaiming, "All lives matter."

Founded by Alicia Garza, Opal Tometi, and Patrisse Cullors, Black Lives Matter[12] is a movement organized to protest violence against black people, specifically, the killing of black men by law enforcement officers.

Black Lives Matter well illustrates how contemporary groups—primarily progressives—ranging from liberal churches, to many individual believers worshipping in evangelical churches and to politicians and the media relate their understanding of "truth-telling." Two assertions regarding #BLM serve to illustrate a typical contemporary perception of 'truth-telling'": (1) Politicians' and the media's lack of effort to try to understand what "truth" means to people who think in progressive/postmodern ways results in a communication breakdown with groups like Black Lives Matter. And (2) A progressive/postmodern understanding of ethical truth, i.e., "truth-telling," is seriously flawed.

The following examples, relating to Black Lives Matter, are used to illustrate "contemporary truth" in a progressive/postmodern context. (*My illustrations are not intended to offer legal opinion or conclusions*).

On July 18, 2015, members of Black Lives Matter "booed" Presidential Candidate (former Maryland Governor), Martin O'Malley for saying, during a campaign rally, "Black lives matter, White lives matter, all lives matter." O'Malley's remark was made in the context of the Governor's announcement of Maryland's appealing of the death penalty under his administration.[13] Why was Governor O'Malley "booed" by members of Black Lives Matter?

10. Watson, "SICK: 'Black Lives Matter' Support Celebrate Murder of Dallas Cops."

11. *Barna Trends, What's New and What's Next at the Intersection of Faith and Culture*, 46.

12. "A Herstory of the #BlackLivesMatter Movement."

13. Governor O'Malley's announcement was very significant. In many capital cases in America, it has been discovered that a high error rate of convictions took place. In twenty-four states, the overall error rate in capital cases were 52% above the average.

INSANITY!

Whereas O'Malley's assertion, "Black lives matter, White lives matter, all lives matter," was not necessarily controversial in a modernist context in which universals (metanarratives) are presupposed and therefore, what is [generally] perceived to be true for one race, is likewise supposed to be true for all races, in a progressive/postmodern context, the message of Black Lives Matter means something very different.

Alicia Garza explains: "Black Lives Matter is an ideological and political intervention in a world where Black lives are systematically and intentionally targeted for demise. It is an affirmation of Black folks' contributions to this society, our humanity, and our resilience in the face of deadly oppression." [14]

For members of Black Lives Matter, their "ideological and political" message is framed in a progressive/postmodern understanding of narrative and therefore, the Black Lives Matter's narrative is founded on a story exclusive to their community; it is intended to express their exclusive "reality" or "truth."

Consequently, in the hearing of members of Black Lives Matter, O'Malley's assertion appeared to ignore BLM's exclusive "reality" or "truth" and consequently, the governor's remark was the equivalence of saying: "I don't believe black men necessarily deserve justice in some exclusive regard." Although Governor O'Malley did not personally intend to offend his audience, his lack of understanding for how members of Black Lives Matter see themselves and relate to their beliefs provoked their "boos."

Governor O'Malley does not stand alone in his lack of understanding. Radio talk show hosts and the media in general consistently misunderstand the *private* or exclusive nature/character of progressive/postmodern "reality" or "truth."

Never-the-less, when properly understood, a progressive/postmodern understanding of ethical truth, "truth-telling," is seriously flawed; particularly concerning the concept and acceptance of "justice" as related in the following tragic examples.

Please observe, the first three examples are on one side of justice; and the latter two examples are on the other side of justice. However, a

---

Twenty-two of the states had overall error rates of 60% or higher. In fifteen states, the error rates were 70% or higher. Maryland, Georgia, Alabama, Mississippi, Oklahoma, Indiana, Wyoming, Montana, Arizona and California have error rates of 75% or higher—"Serious error in capital judgments has reached epidemic proportions," Stassen & Gushee, *Kingdom Ethics*, 212.

14. "A Herstory of the #BlackLivesMatter Movement."

progressive/postmodern understanding of "truth-telling" is incapable of determining "justice" from "injustice."

Eric Garner died in Staten Island, New York City, after an NYPD officer placed him in a chokehold for about 15-19 seconds while arresting him (NYPD policy prohibits the use of a chokehold). The New York City Medical Examiner concluded Garner's death was the result of a combination of the chokehold, compression of his chest, and poor health.[15] The medical examiner ruled Garner's death a homicide.[16] The police officer who administered the chokehold, Officer Pantaleo, was indicted by a grand jury.[17]

A second case briefly considers the death of Laquan McDonald, a seventeen-year-old black youth who was fatally shot by Chicago Police Officer, Jason Van Dyke (Officer Van Dyke shot sixteen rounds into McDonald's body). Police reported that Laquan McDonald was armed with a knife as he was walking diagonally across the street away from police officers when Officer Van Dyke shot and killed him.

McDonald's body jerked repeatedly from the multiple gun shots. The video cam does not show anyone at the scene performing aid on McDonald after the shooting. Officer Van Dyke was charged with first-degree murder on November 24, 2015.[18]

A third case involves Samuel DuBose, an African-American man fatally shot by Ray Tensing, a University of Cincinnati police officer. During a traffic stop for a missing front license plate, Officer Tensing fired on Dubose after he started his car. Officer Tensing stated that as DuBose began to drive off, he was dragged because his arm was caught on the driver's side of the car.

However, prosecutors alleged that footage from Tensing's bodycam showed that he was not dragged. A grand jury indicted Tensing on charges of murder and voluntary manslaughter. Tensing was fired from the police department and a trial date was scheduled.[19]

In each of these three examples, the *prima facie* evidence infers excessive force, criminal activity, on behalf of police officers. If, theoretically, following a trial in which the evidence clearly infers, beyond reasonable

---

15. "Presidential Election, The Road to The White House."

16. According to the medical examiner's definition, a homicide is a death caused by the intentional actions of another person or persons, which is not necessarily and intentional death or a criminal death.

17. "Death of Eric Garner." The City of New York settled with the Garner family for 5.9 million dollars.

18. Laquan McDonald, *re:* Bibliography.

19. Samuel DuBose, *re:* Bibliography.

INSANITY!

doubt, the guilt of the defendant, the police officer, but a jury fails to deliver justice for the plaintiffs, the slain African-American men, then nonviolent public protests demanding justice for these men would most surely be in order.[20]

However, in the case of Michael Brown, the evidence led to the acquittal of Officer Darren Wilson by the United States Department of Justice under President Obama's appointee, Attorney General, Eric Holder.

The shooting of Michael Brown occurred in a northern suburb of St. Louis. Brown was unarmed when he was fatally shot by Officer Wilson. The disputed circumstances surrounding the shooting of Brown sparked violent protests in the predominately black community of Ferguson, Missouri.

Believing that Brown had his hands up and was surrendering himself to Officer Wilson when he was shot, protesters in cities across America chanted, "hands up, don't shoot" as they marched. However, following months of investigation, the U.S. Department of Justice concluded that the "hands up" narrative was founded on false testimony.[21]

My final illustration involves the arrest of Freddy Gray, an African-American man, for possessing what Baltimore Police alleged was an illegal switchblade. While being transported in a police van, Gray fell into a coma and was taken to a trauma center.

Freddy Gray reportedly died from injuries to his spinal cord while being transported in the police van. Pending an investigation, six police officers involved in Gray's arrest and transport were suspended.

The Baltimore City State's Attorney, Marilyn Mosby, announced her office had filed charges against the six police officers after the medical examiner determined Gray's death was a homicide. Violent protests followed Mosby's announcement.

Although a grand jury indicted the six officers on most of Mosby's charges, the first trial ended in a mistrial. And the five remaining defendants were found not guilty of all charges in five separate bench trials by Circuit Judge Barry Williams.[22]

Black Lives Matter however, does not distinguish between justice and injustice; forensic evidence, eyewitness testimony or due process mean

---

20. Again, my intent here is to merely provide examples for illustration of "truth" in a politically correct/postmodern cultural context. I do not intend to play the role of jury and therefore, I strongly urge the reader to research legal opinion beyond my illustrations.

21. Michael Brown, *re:* Bibliography.

22. Freddie Gray, *re:* Bibliography.

nothing. For Black Lives Matter, and an incalculable number of other communities, groups and individuals, "truth," "reality" or "justice" is that which strictly conforms to their uniquely crafted narrative.[23]

Progressive/postmodern "reality" and/or "truth" is seriously flawed for it ultimately provides no grounds for judging between conflicting legal/moral/ethical perspectives and competing narratives. That is, since 'truth" or "reality" is *exclusive* to the narrative created by diverse postmodern communities, a violent gang, a domestic terrorist or a white supremacy group, for example, cannot be morally distinguished from the motives of the Dallas P.D., the Sisters of the Poor or law-abiding American citizens of all races, ethnicities or social-economic standing—*Justice cannot be distinguished from injustice and we are then trapped in a cycle of lawlessness.*

A tragic consequence of progressive/postmodern "reality" and/or "truth" is that Black Lives Matter, among countless other groups and individuals, often end-up promoting the injustice they are otherwise protesting. The demand that their narrative, their version of truth, is acknowledged is not a "two-way street." And it cannot be for it is a narrative crafted in such a way that makes their understanding of "reality" or "truth" *exclusive* to their unique point of view.

Postmodern author Stanley Fish agrees with this conclusion and consequently, the consistent departures from reality of progressive/postmodern "truth": "All preferences are principled, and all principles are preferences . . . .. In short, one person's principles are another person's illegitimate ('mere') preferences."[24] Disparate progressive/postmodern groups/communities then must resign themselves to lawlessness: *"Who's to say what right and wrong is?"*[25]

Living In The Way Of Jesus

> **Mt. 5**—[37] *All you need to say is simply 'Yes' or 'No'; anything beyond this comes from the evil one."* If a believer is living in the simplicity

---

23. *Et. al*, Chapter 2,

24. Fish, *Doing What Comes Naturally:* 11-12.

25. I do not mean to imply that people who hold to a "progressive/postmodern version of truth-telling" are necessarily lawless. Lawlessness begins with our sin-condition. But departures from Biblical "truth-telling," e.g., progressive/postmodern truth-telling, are vulnerable to extremes because of our sinful state, that is, they lead to untruths or departures from reality.

of the faith, they have no need of oaths rather, *"All you need to say is simply 'Yes' or 'No'; anything beyond this comes from the evil one."* Jesus is pointing to personal integrity; oaths are a poor substitute for integrity; and "tolerance" does not equate to truth.

What is Truth? Jesus said: *⁶"I am the way and the truth and the life. No one comes to the Father except through me. ⁷If you really knew me, you would know my Father as well. From now on, you do know him and have seen him"* (John 14:6-7).

Christian truth is *not* founded on an impersonal, abstract cosmic principle but a real Person. Truth is fundamentally who God is—"Anyone who has seen me has seen the Father, said Jesus (Jn. 14:9b). And therefore, *"Everyone on the side of truth listens to me,"* (John 18:37).

If a statement, claim or one's testimony is true, it must conform to God's character—that is, ultimate reality, as revealed in his created order (natural revelation, *et. al.*, chapter 1, "Insanity") and/or special revelation, holy Scripture, the Bible. The Sermon on the Mount, for example, is clear revelation of God's character and how it is to be embodied in narrative form by the church.

When Martin Luther King Jr.'s home was bombed and his family barely escaped serious injury or possibly even death, King courageously displayed kingdom virtue and truth in narrative form as he led the way of nonviolence: "When an angry crowd [of King's supporters] gathered around the King house, armed and calling for vengeance, King sent them home in peace. According to Andrew Young, King's refusal to accept retaliatory violence at that time definitively stamped the character of nonviolence on the civil rights movement. More pointedly, this passion to accept suffering into the self is characteristic of Jesus who was crucified . . .. The letter to the Hebrews tells us that Jesus 'endured the cross, despising the shame' (12:2). And Christians are commanded to take up the cross as Jesus did and to suffer as he suffered."[26]

Racial Reconciliation

What is the church's role in racial reconciliation? Is the church part of the problem today?

---

26. Harak, S.J., *Virtuous Passions: The Formation of Christian Character*, 130-31. In: Stassen & Gushee, 46.

Martin Luther King, Jr. famously said, "It is appalling that the most segregated hour of Christian America is eleven o'clock on Sunday Morning." When all adults were asked if Christian churches were a part of the problem involving racism, 62% "somewhat or strongly disagreed."[27] However, twice as many African-Americans strongly agreed the church was part of the problem (17%) as whites who strongly agreed (9%).[28]

Three-quarters (73%) of American adults believe "Christian churches play an important role in racial reconciliation."[29] 94% of Evangelicals believe Christian Churches participate in very significant ways towards racial reconciliation in America.[30]

However, Brooke Hempell, vice president of research for the Barna Group states: "This research confirms the fear that the Church . . . may be part of the problem in the hard work of racial reconciliation."[31] Hempell is referring to the fact that if a person is a white, evangelical Republican, they are less likely to see racism as a problem; instead, they are more likely to see themselves as a victim of reverse racism. They also apparently refuse to acknowledge that a person of color is socially disadvantaged in contemporary America.[32] And yet, "these same groups believe the Church plays an important role in reconciliation."[33] If you are white, an evangelical and a Republican, you may be vulnerable to "blind-spots" when it comes to the plight of both African-American believers and unbelievers.

A failure to acknowledge bias ("blind-spots") leads to peoples disconnect from the reality of, in this case, the struggles of African-Americans and consequently, white Christians may not even be aware that they are perpetuating "the divisions, inequalities, and injustices that prevent African American communities from thriving."[34]

In June 1963, President John F. Kennedy unveiled plans to pursue a comprehensive civil rights bill in Congress, stating, "this nation, for all its

---

27. *Barna Trends, 2017,* 46.

28. Ibid.

29. Ibid. An apparent trend is that the older someone is the more they believe the church plays an important role in racial reconciliation: Millennials, 66%; Gen-Xers, 69%; Boomers, 79%; and Elders, 84%.

30. Ibid., 47.

31. Ibid.

32. Ibid.

33. Ibid.

34. Ibid.

hopes and all its boasts, will not be fully free until all its citizens are free." Martin Luther King Jr. congratulated Kennedy on his pursuit of a comprehensive civil rights bill calling it "one of the most eloquent, profound and unequivocal pleas for justice and the freedom of all men ever made by any president."[35] *But since 1963, post-Christian notions of truth, justice and freedom (e.g., progressive/postmodern) have served to create increasing levels of racial division and hostility in American life and consequently, rather than progressing, we have digressed as a culture.*

Spiritual Formation

1. *What does "freedom" mean in relation to American exceptionalism? What does "freedom" mean without form? Was Martin Luther King Jr.'s understanding of "freedom" with or without form? How did King's understanding of "freedom" influence his nonviolent approach to Civil Rights?*

2. *What are your criteria for truth? In other words, how do you test someone's assertion, claim, or testimony to discover if it is true or not?*

3. *How important to the cause of Christ is a "normative" understanding (an understanding founded on primary sources) of the "other side's" worldview?*

4. *How do the Ten Commandments (Exodus 20:1-17/Deuteronomy 5:6-21) reflect both God's character and criteria for truth, justice and freedom?*

---

35. "Martin Luther King Jr. And the Global Freedom Struggle, Civil Rights Acts, 1964."

Chapter 7

'An Eye for an Eye'—Revenge

Matthew 5:38-42

By means of our obedience to "the way of Jesus," we see Christian values, throughout history, subverting pagan values in radical ways.

> **Matthew 5:38-42**—[38] "You have heard that it was said, 'Eye for eye, and tooth for tooth.' [39] But I tell you, do not resist an evil person. If anyone slaps you on the right cheek, turn to them the other cheek also. [40] And if anyone wants to sue you and take your shirt, hand over your coat as well. [41] If anyone forces you to go one mile, go with them two miles. [42] Give to the one who asks you, and do not turn away from the one who wants to borrow from you.

The Mosaic law was both civil and moral. The Ten Commandments (Ex. 20), for example, prescribe moral law for Israelites to follow; and Exodus 21-23 involves civil law, the moral standards of the Ten Commandments are applied to the social life of the nation.

Stott observes that in relation to the variety of "case-laws" discussed in Exodus 21-23, the following language is used: "When men strive together . . . if any harm follows, then you shall give life for life, eye for eye, tooth for tooth, hand for hand, foot for foot, burn for burn, wound for wound, stripe for stripe."[1] This is the type of language used for Israel's civil law. Israel's civil law was intended to both define justice and restrain vengeance;

---

1. Re: Ex. 21:22-25, *Cf.* Lv. 24:19, 20; Dt. 19:21. Stott, *The Message of the Sermon on the Mount*, 104.

"It also prohibited the taking of the law into one's own hands by the ghastly vengeance of the family feud."[2]

But the teachers of the law, the scribes and the Pharisees, redefined the "principle of just retribution" strictly intended for judges to apply through the courts, and instead used it as justification for personal revenge.

The Pharisees' perversion of the law prompted Jesus' correction: [38]*"You have heard that it was said, 'Eye for eye, and tooth for tooth.'* [39] *But I tell you, do not resist an evil person."* The Scripture literally says, "But I say to you not to oppose the evil one."

Since we are consistently told by different New Testament authors to "oppose" the "evil one," Satan (*cf.* Eph. 6:13; 1 Pet. 5:9; Jas. 4:7), the Devil is not the object of Jesus' command. Rather, "... we are forbidden to resist ... not evil as such, evil in the abstract, ... but an evil person, *one who is evil* ...."[3] The command, "do not *resist* an evil person," explicitly means "...do not retaliate revengefully by evil means."[4]

A Not So Subtle Conflict Between Values

"The way we learn something is more influential than the something that we learn. No content comes into our lives free-floating: it is always embedded in a form of some kind. For the basic integrative realities of God and faith, the forms must also be basic and integrative. If they are not, the truths themselves will be peripheral and unassimilated"—Eugene Peterson.

"When the Anglo-Saxons in England adopted Christianity," observes C. John Sommerville, "they may not have entirely understood what they were buying into. The values their leaders had always found self-evident were the values associated with the concept of honor, which means earning and insisting on respect from others. By contrast, the values self-evident to the Christian missionaries were the values of charity, meaning wanting the best for others."[5]

2. Ibid.

3. Ibid., 105.

4. Stassen and Gushee grammatically point out that this is not a Greek imperative but an infinitive—"probably with implied imperatival meaning," that is, Jesus' directive or command is implied, *Kingdom Politics,* 137.

5. Sommerville, *The Decline of the Secular University,* 69. The Anglo-Saxons inhabited Great Britain from the 5th century. They originated as Germanic tribes that migrated to Great Britain from continental Europe. The Anglo-Saxon period in British

For those whose values associated with honor and respect are self-evident—that is, they were learned in nonreflective ways through modeling by parents and society, their moral behavior was [is] compelled by personal recognition: "What can I do that will bring me honor and respect from my peers and superiors?" Therefore, a person motivated by honor and respect may do a kind thing for someone in need *if* their act will promote their reputation as an honorable person and gain the respect of others. *Their ethic is then self-regarding.*

The values self-evident to the Christian missionaries, contrary to the Anglo-Saxons, were those associated with charity; they were motivated by an "*other-regarding ethic*" and consequently, they were not concerned with recognition of their achievements or legacy but rather with what is best for others.

Contrary to the Anglo-Saxons, the values of the Christian missionaries were integrated into their lives following conversion and the sanctifying process of daily conforming their lives to Christ's character. The values [virtues] of the kingdom of God are supremely modeled in Jesus Christ.

Values founded on honor and respect and values founded on charity are equally self-evident for the people who are shaped by them. But Sommerville stresses that with ". . . honor goes a concentration on pride rather than humility, dominance rather than service, courage rather than peaceableness, glory rather than modesty, loyalty rather than respect for all, generosity to one's friends rather than equality. Charity expresses the contrasting values in each of these pairs."[6]

Therefore, the Anglo-Saxons were very slow to apprehend the values of the Christian missionaries; they could not understand how any culture that did not embrace strength could survive. But the problem was/is that the self-regarding values of the Anglo-Saxons uncritically made honor, respect and strength an end-in-themselves instead of Christ, who is paradoxically Almighty God, "the Lion of the tribe of Judah, the root of David, [who] has triumphed" (Rev. 5:5b); and One who is meek and gentle, the Lamb, "who was slain" (Rev. 5:6; 12).

The Anglo-Saxons then "twisted Christianity into something that could preach the Crusades, which were to protect God's honor;"[7]

history was between about 450 to 1066.
  6. Ibid., 70.
  7. Ibid.

INSANITY!

Anglo-Saxon values persuaded the church to "seize the sword" (cf. Rom. 13:4) and go to war "in the name of Christ."[8]

Living In The Way Of Jesus

> **Mt. 5—**[39]*"If anyone slaps you on the right cheek, turn to them the other cheek also.* [40] *And if anyone wants to sue you and take your shirt, hand over your coat as well.* [41] *If anyone forces you to go one mile, go with them two miles.* [42] *Give to the one who asks you, and do not turn away from the one who wants to borrow from you".*

People shaped by values championing pride, dominance and self-glorification, that is, the values of the Anglo-Saxons, would undoubtedly hear Jesus' words, *"If anyone slaps you on the right cheek, turn to them the other cheek also"* as weakness, submissiveness and/or compromise.

But, in the first-century Palestinian cultural context, it was forbidden for anyone to slap another with the left hand; the left hand was for unclean or dirty things.[9] The "turning of the other cheek" would have surprised the offender and gained their attention to hear, without words, "you are treating me as an unequal, but I need to be treated as an equal." Jesus is saying, "if you are slapped on the cheek of inferiority, turn the cheek of equal dignity."[10] Verses 39b–42 equate to a nonviolent protest founded on human dignity and equality; *a person unwilling to hear such a protest is him or herself a dishonorable person unworthy of respect.*

How can Jesus' imperative to "turn the other cheek" practically produce cultural-transformation in America? Martin Luther King Jr., for example, confronted white racism and inequality by means of "turning the other cheek." King's marches were nonviolent; and they conscientiously [and properly so] made human dignity, particularly, the dignity of African-Americans, an end-in-itself.

---

8. My explanation is intended to relate strictly to the influence of Anglo-Saxon values on the thinking of Christians; it is not intended to say anything about Christian ethics and war. For discussion concerning Christian ethics and war, see for example, Stassen & Gushee, *Kingdom Ethics*, "Just War, Nonviolence and Just Peacemaking;" Kaiser, *Toward Old Testament Ethics*; Harrison, *Encyclopedia of Biblical and Christian Ethics*; and Jersild and Johnson, *Moral Issues and Christian Response, Third Edition.*

9. Stassen, *Kingdom Ethics*, 139.

10. Ibid.

King's *means* acknowledged human dignity, that is, the *means* employed by King were nonviolent towards other image-bearers and their property, and the *ends* (as alluded to above) concluded in the demand for equal dignity among Whites, Blacks and all races. King's obedience to Jesus' sermon transformed American politics and culture and resulted in the Civil Rights Act in 1964, ending segregation, and the Voting Rights Act for African-Americans in 1965.

Paul instructs an ancient church in righteousness: *Do not be overcome by evil, but overcome evil with good.*[11] By means of our obedience to "the way of Jesus," we see Christian values, throughout history, subverting pagan values in radical ways; the most extreme example is the cross used by pagans to execute criminals but used by God to save sinners (Acts 4:8-12).

Spiritual Formation

1. *What is the primary theme in this chapter?*
2. *What are some Biblical examples of a "self-regarding ethic" and an "other regarding ethic"?*
3. *How is Paul's exhortation for us to: "Honor one another above yourselves" (Rom. 12:10b) different from the Anglo-Saxon notion of "honor"?*
4. *Regarding the Crusades, how was the church persuaded to disregard Jesus' application of the law and rather embrace a pharisaic version of an "eye for an eye"?*
5. *Does Jesus' teaching necessarily teach pacifism relative to war?*

---

11. Romans 12:21.

Chapter 8

'Love Your Enemies'

Matthew 5:43-48

IF, BEGINNING ON THE cultural margins, the Sermon on the Mount takes narrative form in a minority of God's covenant people, incivility and lawlessness in local communities will be countered—"It is living-in-truth that proves culturally powerful."[1]

N.T. Wright shares a story of Aleksandr Solzhenitsyn's return to Russia after twenty years of exile. During his journey, Solzhenitsyn greeted his fellow citizens in every town. However, he also greeted former Communist officials who themselves had tyrannized many of Solzhenitsyn's fellow citizens. In response to objections from some of his fellow Russians to his kind gestures towards these officials, Solzhenitsyn protested saying, "the line between good and evil is never simply between 'us' and 'them.' The line between good and evil runs through each one of us."[2]

A Deeply Divided Nation

Leading up to the 1970's and preceding decades, the bell curve— —defined normal (norms) as centralized rather than to one extreme or the other. Most people [were] average regarding life skills, academic performance, athletic ability, professional achievement, personal appearance; and as having a small or large family.

---

1. Guinness, *Renaissance, The Power of the Gospel However Dark the Times*, 75.
2. Wright, *Evil and the Justice of God*, 38.

Most people [were] more "centered," albeit, left or right centered, regarding social, religious and political/ideological points of view. In other words, although we saw ourselves as adversaries; and our collective sense of human dignity was quickly fading, civil dialogue was still, on varying levels, achievable.

The emergent culture in the mid1980's and into the 21st century ushered in an *ideological pluralism*. An ideological pluralism is marked by peoples' political or social views becoming their personal identity.[3]

"Normal" was then redefined by an inverted bell curve or "well-curve"— ⌣ . The well-curve sees the majority population gravitating to the extremes, resulting in the political, ideological and social polarization of U.S. American culture.

On the "Left" are progressive secularists, socialist Democrats, the liberal church, pro-choice activists, pro-active euthanasia (doctor-assisted-suicide), same-sex marriage, #Black-Lives-Matter, anti-2nd Amendment rights, open borders, Antifa (Anti-fascism) and anarchists (the former "Occupy Movement"—"Occupy L.A., Portland, Minneapolis," etc. appear to have morphed into these even more extreme left wing views); and the triumph of "Tolerance" over the freedom of personal conscience, that is, Religious Liberty—Cultural Marxism's influence is ubiquitous on the left.

And on the "Right" is free-enterprise, capitalism; traditionalist Independent conservatives, the Tea Party, a lot of angry Republicans; pro-life advocates; traditional male-female marriage, closed borders, cultural assimilation, pro-2nd Amendment rights, many aligned with the evangelical church. And, on the extreme right is "Alt-Right" and white supremacy groups.

Our nation politically, ideologically and socially is polarized to the point of breaking; confusion dominates every layer of our culture and with each passing day, the sentiment on both sides becomes increasingly hostile; *America's ideological, political and social polarization creates a cultural condition wherein "society is absolute."* The line between good and evil profoundly separates "us" from "them" and each side hates the other!

---

3. Unlike social pluralism, which is an observable phenomenon consisting of a variety of disparate worldviews, religions, and social classes intermixing in relative ways, an "ideological pluralism" results when different factions of the population make their political or social point of view their personal identity—that is, "truth" or "reality" in the context of an ideological pluralism is founded on the identity of each community or party instead of God or a personal Transcendent outside the flux of historical/cultural patterns and change—*Society, that is the different factions, are is/then Absolute.*

INSANITY!

But why has the evangelical church chosen sides? A significant portion of evangelical Christians have been enticed into believing that politics is capable of solving pre-political cultural problems.[4] But James Davison Hunter uncovers a stark reality: The culturally conservative side of the Evangelical Church bets "on politics as the means to respond to the changes in the world, but that politics can only be a losing strategy. What political solution is there to the absence of decency? To the spread of vulgarity? To the lack of civility and the want of compassion? The answer, of course, is none—there are no political solutions to these concerns, and the headlong pursuit of them by conservatives will lead, inevitably, to failure."[5]

Politics, for "all its gritty realism is the proper calling of lay people. . . . Christians should be engaged in politics, but never equated without remainder with any party or ideology."[6] By choosing sides, that is, by becoming "equated without remainder with any party or ideology," a mass number of evangelical Christians have actually created a counter-productive environment to their otherwise sincere cause to rescue our culture.

The Religious Left initiated the unsavory practice of "politicizing" the faith in the 1960s. And in the late 1970s, the Religious Right followed the Left in this grave error of "using faith to express essentially political points that have lost touch with biblical truth."[7] The result of the "politicizing of the faith" is the framing of Christian faith in the ideology of a political party, "Christian faith becomes an ideology in its purest form: Christian beliefs are used as weapons for political interests."[8] *And consequently, rather than striving together as "one nation under God," we now seek to justify our vindictive attitudes by conforming the divine law to our ideological/political ends.*

'The Line Between Good And Evil'

> Mt. 5—[43] "You have heard that it was said, 'Love your neighbor and hate your enemy.' [44] But I tell you, love your enemies and pray for those who persecute you, [45] that you may be children of your

---

4. Guinness, *The Case for Civility*, 100.

5. Hunter and Wolfe, *Is There a Culture War?* 95. In: Guinness, *The Case for Civility*, 101.

6. Ibid., 100.

7. Ibid.

8. Ibid.

> Father in heaven. He causes his sun to rise on the evil and the good, and sends rain on the righteous and the unrighteous. *⁴⁶ If you love those who love you, what reward will you get? Are not even the tax collectors doing that? ⁴⁷ And if you greet only your own people, what are you doing more than others? Do not even pagans do that? ⁴⁸ Be perfect, therefore, as your heavenly Father is perfect."*

"Love your enemies:" here is the highest point on the mount and at the same time, the lowest point in the valley. The Sermon on the Mount is as admired as it is resented at this point. Martin Luther King Jr. gives rare insight: "Jesus understood the difficulty inherent in the act of loving one's enemy . . . . He realized that every genuine expression of love grows out of a consistent and total surrender to God."[9]

The same One, who while bleeding out on the Cross, interceded for those who made themselves his enemies, "Father, forgive them, for they do not know what they are doing" (Luke 23:34), requires believers to expand our circle of love to include those who persecute us: *"In practicing this kind of love, we are 'children of our Father in heaven.'"*[10] But how do believers "live out" this kind of love?

Living In The Way Of Jesus

"Be perfect, therefore, as your heavenly Father is perfect." Is Jesus requiring moral perfection from us? No, not at all, the Greek word translated "perfect" (*teleioi*) means *complete* in a moral sense of love; love includes all, even enemies.[11] This is the point that Jesus emphasizes in this teaching: "the love of God's grace that includes the complete circle of humankind, with enemies in it as well, by contrast with tax collectors and Gentiles, who love only their friends."[12]

A kingdom ethic is most outstandingly marked by sacrificial love, that is, interpreting and living life by way of the Cross. In practicing this kind of love, instead of choosing sides, Biblical Christians live with the conviction that "the line between good and evil is never simply between 'us' and 'them.' The line between good and evil runs through each one of us." Loving one's enemies compels a believer to act as "peacemaker" rather than taking sides.

9. Luther King, Jr., *Strength to Love*, 48.
10. Stassen & Gushee, *Kingdom Ethics*, 140-141.
11. BAGD, 809.
12. Stassen & Gushee, *Kingdom Ethics*, 141.

INSANITY!

As secularization metastasizes, the post-Christian west is increasingly turning itself over to the corrupting effects of paganism—*Our post-Christian culture "nearly universally celebrates" the perversion of the created order* (*et. al.*, Romans 1:18-32).

Our culture's lawlessness is fast-approaching a tipping point when the "social chaos will be beyond recovery."[13] How then should the church respond to America's ideological, political and social polarization?

The Church In Exile

John Mark Comer is a pastor and author living in a city wherein the corrosive effects of secularization have reached a tipping point. But rather than expensive marketing schemes designed to attract "not-yet-Christians" to his church, Pastor Comer has chosen to actively join his city, Portland, Oregon, in its exile: "The task of the church in an exile-like setting is to rediscover the teachings of Jesus and the practices of the early church, then apply them to the corrosive soil of a Western secularized city—like Portland or San Francisco or New York or L.A."[14]

If the Sermon on the Mount took narrative form in God's covenant people, that is, if a local church rediscovered "the teachings of Jesus and the practices of the early church," and applied them "to the corrosive soil" of America's secularized culture, what would a "Western secularized city" see?

Joing American Culture In Exile

Micah 6:8 is revelation of an answer: *"And what does the Lord require of you? To act justly and to love mercy and to walk humbly with your God."*

We are *"to act justly;"* or *"do justice;" "act"* or *"do"* are verbs, we are required to obediently engage justice. The Hebrew term translated "act justly" (*mispat*) finds "its source in God himself and therefore carrying with it his demand."[15] In the Old Testament, this term (*mispat*) is connected to: widows, orphans, the poor, the needy, the oppressed, the stranger, the prisoner,

---

13. Ibid.

14. Pastor, (Interview) "John Mark Comer, The Westside: Bridgetown," *Outreach Magazine.com*, The 2016 Outreach 100, 33.

15. Harris, Archer, Jr., and Waltke, *Theological Wordbook of the Old Testament*, Vol. II (Chicago, IL.: Moody Press, 1980), 948-49.

and the fatherless.[16] To "act justly" connects the believer to people living on the extreme margins of culture. *Our relationship with God directly relates to how we care for these people.*

The most effective strategy for transformation, at least on the large scale that the kingdom of God involves, comes from a minority in whose lives the Sermon on the Mount is taking narrative form; and having "heard the call to be missional," [17] they are working from the margins to the center.

To "walk humbly" emphasizes spiritual preparation, *what we do;* to *"love mercy"* focuses on the believer's heart, *who we are.* "Christ in us" compels us, as a new humanity, to "love mercy." The Hebrew term (*hesed*) is related to our understanding of "compassion." The Latin understanding is more precise however: we are to *"co-suffer, to come alongside of"* the hurting, the weak, the vulnerable and the poor.

To love mercy, you must be where the pain is, because God is hidden in the pain. By throwing yourself into a place of pain, you discover the joy of Jesus. All ministry in the history of the church is built on a vision of *holistic redemption,* that is, ministry is committed to the common good of the culture by its unashamed, single-minded commitment to the Cross, and the dynamic power of the Holy Spirit's presence in the lives of believers.

Ministry is for helping people discover that in the middle of pain there is hope and blessing. In our world, there is an enormous distinction between good and bad, sorrow and joy. But in God's eyes, they are never separated: where there is pain, there is healing; where there is mourning, there is dancing; and where there is poverty, there is the riches of the kingdom.

And God requires us to: *"walk humbly."* The Hebrew term translated "walk humbly" literally means, "creating space." We are to "create space" or environments in which God can act.

We are to see the staggering needs in our world and acknowledge that God is before all other things in our lives: ourselves, our family, our friends, our life's goals and aspirations, our personal security and comfort, *everything.* We are called to take the place of others and see the physical and spiritual needs in our community and the world and ask ourselves: *"What can I do for the person I see across the street, across my office space, on my work site, across the world?"*[18]

---

16. Brown, Driver, and Briggs, *Hebrew and English Lexicon,* (490), 48; (3490), 450, (1800), 195, (34), 2, (7533), 954, (1616), 158, (615/16), 64, (3490), 450.

17. Belcher, *Deep Church, A Third Way Beyond Emerging and Traditional,* 203.

18. My thoughts are inspired by Paul Hurkman, *Venture Expeditions,* contained in a

INSANITY!

If the Sermon on the Mount took narrative form in God's covenant people, that is, if a local church rediscovered "the teachings of Jesus and the practices of the early church," and applied them "to the corrosive soil" of America's secularized culture, what would a "Western secularized city" see?

They would see the "kingdom which Jesus came to bring on earth as in heaven [taking] root in, and [being] implemented through, the cleansed and softened hearts of his followers."[19] They would see God's covenant people incarnating the peace (*shālōm*) of God and practically expressing it by loving their enemies through justice, mercy and humility (cf. Micah 6:8).

If, beginning on the cultural margins, the Sermon on the Mount takes narrative form in a minority of God's covenant people, incivility, lawlessness and even insanity in local communities will be countered—"It is living-in-truth that proves culturally powerful."

Spiritual Formation

1. What is the central theme of this chapter?
2. How can the local church transform the culture around it?
3. What are some biblical examples and contemporary examples of the body of Christ "creating environments" for God to act?
4. In your opinion, what is the greatest danger to contemporary America?
5. How should the church respond to America's ideological, political, and social polarization? Is the US American church prepared to obey Jesus' command to "love your enemies," even far-left or post-Christian liberals?

---

sermon delivered at Cedar Valley Church, Bloomington, MN., January 13, 2013.

19. Wright, *After You Believe, Why Christian Character Matters*, 123.

Chapter 9

'When You Give'

Matthew 6:1-4

"Give, and it will be given to you. A good measure, pressed down, shaken together and running over, will be poured into your lap. For with the measure you use, it will be measured to you," Luke 6:38.

6—[1] *"Be careful not to practice your righteousness in front of others to be seen by them. If you do, you will have no reward from your Father in heaven.* [2] *"So when you give to the needy, do not announce it with trumpets, as the hypocrites do in the synagogues and on the streets, to be honored by others. Truly I tell you, they have received their reward in full.* [3] *But when you give to the needy, do not let your left hand know what your right hand is doing,* [4] *so that your giving may be in secret. Then your Father, who sees what is done in secret, will reward you."*

THE THREE PILLARS OF Jewish piety,[1] "When you give," "When you pray," and "When you fast" now follow in Jesus' sermon. "When you give," give with anonymity to God's kingdom and righteousness; anonymity punctuates true righteousness: *"Be careful not to practice your righteousness in front of others to be seen by them"* . . . *"do not announce it with trumpets"* . . . *"do not let your left hand know what your right hand is doing."* The believer's faithfulness to these holy practices, when done in secret, that is, righteously, will be rewarded by God, our Father (6:1; 6:6; 6:18b).

---

1. Gundry, *Matthew*, 101.

INSANITY!

"Rooster Cogburn"

In the spirit of the poor widow who put two small copper coins in the treasury, "all she had to live on" (Lk. 21: 2), so also, a poor Kenyan family humbly gave a rooster out of their poverty to Matt and Cheryl Tallman, missionaries to Kenya. Matt Tallman's amazing story (in his words) of how God measures a good gift follows.

> Many people wonder in a world with billions of people that don't know Jesus, what difference giving a missions' gift or making a missions' pledge will do. I didn't fully realize this myself until Cheryl and I moved to Kenya in 2009 to work at an AIDS orphanage with Open Arms International. Soon after we moved to Eldoret, Kenya, we were invited to speak at a rural church; we arrived at a small mud structure filled with nearly 300 people, eager to hear us speak.
>
> Shortly after I stood up to speak, I noticed that human beings were not the only inhabitants of this humble church building. There was also a small herd of goats and sheep, and about three dozen chickens and roosters. As I continued to speak some of the chickens flew over the heads of the congregation, but it didn't make sense to me until they took up the offering at the end of the service. That was the offering. In rural Africa, no one has a paying job; they live off-of subsistence farming, and that is all they have to give: eggs, vegetables, sheep, goats, chickens, and roosters.
>
> At the very end of the service, the elders of the church asked the pastor what they should give the guest speaker. I didn't expect anything but was humbled and honored that they insisted on giving us a rooster. They lined up the dozen roosters in the offering and said, "pick the best one". While this rooster may seem like a modest gift, it represented a significant sacrifice from the families of that church who literally gave up a meal to give us that rooster. We placed the rooster in a cardboard box and wondered what we were going to do with this creature when we got back to our little children's village in Eldoret.
>
> Fortunately, one of our Kenyan house parents had the foresight to build a hen house at our village a few days before this to help provide fresh eggs for the village. He suggested that we put this rooster in the hen house and a few weeks later I noticed that there were a few baby chickens running around the hen house. I talked with the house parents, and Rachel Gallagher, the co-founder of the village, and suggested that maybe we could build a separate chicken coop and raise broiler chickens to eat. A local

lady in the community heard about our new broiler project and wanted to contribute dozens of her own baby chicks to help get this new project started. I am not a farmer, but somehow within three months we were harvesting 50 chickens every other week and our egg production had already tripled.

We quickly began raising more chickens than we could possibly eat at the village, so we started going into town and selling the chickens in local grocery stores and restaurants. There was a good market for chickens in which we could make a net profit of a $1.50 per chicken. We began building more chicken coops and soon we were harvesting nearly 1000 chickens per month and laying nearly 1000 eggs per day. All the chickens and eggs now feed our entire village with 150 AIDS orphans, their house parents, our staff, 225 additional children in our 2 schools, and over 400 more children in our daily feeding program. In addition, the excess chickens and eggs we sell pay for the salaries of several of our full time Kenyan staff.

We soon began to dream of the possibility of making this village completely self-sustainable and think about other projects that could help make our village financially self-supporting. As we approach our goals of sustainability, we have also begun dreaming about the possibility of replicating this village in other parts of East Africa.

This is a wonderful dream, and it is exciting to see it become a reality, but it should not be forgotten that it all began with the gift of one rooster, from one family, in one poor, rural Kenyan church, that literally had no money, but they gave from what they had…one rooster.

When you think about what difference one missions pledge or one missions gift can make in this world, think of the gift of one rooster (A John Wayne fan, Matt decided to name this special rooster, "Rooster Cogburn") and what a difference it has already made in Kenya, "For with the measure you use"—A Kenyan family's measure was "all they had to live on"—"it will be measured to" an entire community and is literally "running over" onto increasing numbers of African children daily![2]

---

2. Matt & Cheryl Tallman are missionaries to Kenya through Open Arms International—www.OpenArmsInternational.com.

INSANITY!
Living In The Way Of Jesus

"So when you give to the needy..."

Images of poverty, and the poor, are stitched into the larger fabric of the prophets' and the apostles' interpretation of God's historical self-disclosure, especially his humiliation through the Incarnation. For this reason, Christ's humiliation and poverty (2 Cor. 8:9) confront us with the poor who remind us of our spiritual poverty (*et. al.*, Mt. 5:3). Throughout the history of the church, those who have been beneficiaries of the grace of God have been called to reveal Christ's poverty to their neighbors: the poor, the vulnerable, and the disenfranchised.[3]

In a just society, the perpetuation of poverty is not tolerated (Isa. 10:1-4; 58:3-12, Jer. 5:26-29; 22:13-19, Amos 2:6-7; 4:1-3; 5:10-15). Educational systems, hospitals, orphanages, care for the poor, the homeless, widows, the dying, the mentally handicapped, and visiting the imprisoned have their origins in the Gospel—*Historically, the church has been the only entity on earth that exists for the benefit of all of its nonmembers.*[4]

Imago Dei, located on Portland's eastside, is an extraordinary example of a church "that exists for the benefit of all of its nonmembers." Imago Dei's website asks:

> What would it take for a neighborhood to be transformed by the gospel of Jesus Christ? As the people of God we eat, sleep, work in the garden, talk over the fence, patronize businesses, and take the kids to school in neighborhoods. That's pretty normal and could be temporal and fairly insignificant—unless you're traveling along on the missional journey of God. In that case it all takes on an eternal significance. The difference is determined by conscious awareness and cooperation with Jesus who is leading this journey. Where is he leading? Could it be into neighborhoods? Might he

---

3. Resources and agencies willing to work with the church for the common good abound in American communities. Correctional systems openly welcome Christian ministry into the prison system. State and county government is willing to work alongside the church to provide care for AIDS/HIV victims. Drug and alcohol treatment agencies and centers are responsive to the church's offer to come alongside of them. CASA, Court Appointed Special Advocates, places and supervises children in foster homes. CASA is open to Christians and churches helping in the placement and supervision process.

4. Archbishop William Temple is cited for this observation in *Towards an Evangelical Public Policy*, 232.

lead us to live in a particular neighborhood where we intentionally journey in mission for the sake of our neighbors?[5]

Imago Dei identifies "aching places" in the city of Portland and calls its members together to discuss, connect and pray about some of them relocating to the aching places; and redistributing resources for the common good in the aching places, and reconciling an aching neighborhood or business district to Christ's unconditional love.

Imago Dei makes disciples of not-yet-Christians by being the presence of Christ for them. Imago Dei's founder, and lead pastor, Rick McKinley, measures success in missional terms: *"If we ever left, would this city miss us?"*[6] Pastor McKinley's metric of success compels him to see the church *"existing for the sake of the world, not for itself."*[7]

Brian Zimmerman is the Lead Pastor of Street-Lite Christian Fellowship in Baltimore, Maryland. Embedded in the description of Street-Life Christian Fellowship ministry is a reference to Luke 4: *"Jesus said that He came to 'preach the gospel to the poor, proclaim release to the captives, sight to the blind, and freedom to the downtrodden.' Jesus came to 'proclaim the favorable year of the Lord!'"* [8]

Three questions surface when a believer reads Jesus' description of the purpose of his ministry: Where is Jesus? What is he doing? And how can we join him?

The mission and vision of Street-Lite Fellowship is daily fulfilled as they faithfully join Jesus on the margins of "one of the most dangerous cities in the United States" and ". . . passionately and holistically address the felt needs and the spiritual emptiness in [their] community, Baltimore, and [their] world through the vehicle of surrendered Street-Lite members and strategic partners who are using their time, treasure, and talents to transform lives for Christ." [9] Like Imago Dei on the West Coast, Street-Lite Fellowship exists on the East Coast, *"for the sake of the world, not for itself."*

---

5. Imago Dei Community: http://www.imagodeicommunity.com, 11/15/2007.
6. Pastor, *Outreach*, "Rick McKinley, The Eastside: Imago Dei," 36.
7. Ibid.
8. http://www.streetlite.com/who-we-are/our-vision/
9. Ibid.

INSANITY!

Spiritual Formation

1. *What is the central theme of this chapter?*
2. *How does righteousness relate to the three main pillars of Jewish piety?*
3. *Do you have a testimony to share of how God miraculously provided for you and your family in a time of need?*
4. *How do the poor remind us of our spiritual poverty? How does the understanding of our spiritual poverty relate to spiritual power in our lives?*

Chapter 10

'When You Pray'

Matthew 6:5-14

"When you make a request to God in prayer, God will always give you exactly what you would have asked for if you knew everything he knows about your life and situation"

—Timothy Keller.

Mt. 6—[5] *"And when you pray, do not be like the hypocrites, for they love to pray standing in the synagogues and on the street corners to be seen by others. Truly I tell you, they have received their reward in full.* [6] *But when you pray, go into your room, close the door and pray to your Father, who is unseen. Then your Father, who sees what is done in secret, will reward you.* [7] *And when you pray, do not keep on babbling like pagans, for they think they will be heard because of their many words.* [8] *Do not be like them, for your Father knows what you need before you ask him.* [9] *"This, then, is how you should pray:*

"'Our Father in heaven,
hallowed be your name,
[10] *your kingdom come,*
your will be done,
    on earth as it is in heaven.
[11] *Give us today our daily bread.*
[12] *And forgive us our debts,*
    as we also have forgiven our debtors.

INSANITY!

> ¹³ *And lead us not into temptation,*
> *but deliver us from the evil one.'*
> ¹⁴ *For if you forgive other people when they sin against you, your heavenly Father will also forgive you.* ¹⁵ *But if you do not forgive others their sins, your Father will not forgive your sins."*

PRAYER, IN PARALLEL WITH the other two "pillars of Jewish piety," giving to the needy and fasting, is characterized by anonymity: *⁵ "And when you pray, do not be like the hypocrites, for they love to pray standing in the synagogues and on the street corners to be seen by others. Truly I tell you, they have received their reward in full."*

The anonymity of Christian prayer is contrary to the hypocrites' public spectacle, for the sake of recognition, which is their empty reward. (Jesus is not referring to public prayer, cf. Mt. 18:19-20; 1 Tim. 2:8, but prayer motivated by self-seeking glory).

Jesus also tells his disciples: *⁷ And when you pray, do not keep on babbling like pagans, for they think they will be heard because of their many words.* The Greek term translated, "babbling" (NIV) means: "speak without thinking."[1] The pagans (Gentiles) thought they could manipulate their deities by heaping up "empty phrases" (RSV).

Pagans also attempted to hold their deities to "contractual obligations" by reminding them of favors they owed to their devotees.[2] Christians, Jew and Gentile, are in covenant relationship with God, not some contractual agreement: "One may note that whereas ancient Israel shared with its neighbors thank offerings, atonement offerings and so forth, Israel had no sacrifices to secure rain or any favors from God; God gave these blessings only in response to Israel's obedience to his covenant (Deut. 27-18)."[3]

The vivid contrast between the motives of the Pharisees, the "hypocrites," who seek their own glory and the senseless babbling of pagans (heathen Gentiles) prepares the human heart to hear of a third way, the Christian way of prayer. The Christian way of prayer is secret, simple and deeply experiential.

Notice the connection between "secret" and "reward" in verse 6: *⁶ "But when you pray, go into your room, close the door and pray to your Father, who is unseen. Then your Father, who sees what is done in secret, will reward*

---

1. BAGD, 137.
2. Keener, *Matthew*, 139.
3. Ibid.

you." As we pray in this way, God lovingly comes into our lives where our deepest cares are; his intimate presence overshadows us.[4]

"Give Us Today Our Daily Bread"

My first lead pastorate was in a small logging town in southwestern Washington. From its inception in 1924, my little church had experienced several splits and pastors remained only a short time; the church had had 48 different senior pastors from 1924-1980.

Following its most recent split, the church was left with 25 people. The annual church budget was 16 thousand dollars a year. My salary was $100 a week and a parsonage (the parsonage was in desperate need of repair; daylight appeared in several places through one wall).

Early into our ministry, we had absolutely no money and we were literally out of food. And although our little church had very loving people in it, I did not think of asking them for help.

On a Friday evening, my wife and I prayed and asked the Lord to provide dinner for our daughters. We then decided to set the table as though we had food for dinner. Our oldest daughter asked where our dinner was; our daughters did not know that we had nothing to eat.

We prayed together and gave God thanks for his faithfulness to us. As I closed in prayer, the doorbell rang. I went to the door but no one was there. A large black kettle, two smaller pots and a loaf of bread had been placed on the small wooden steps. A pair of pot holders had also been placed beside the pots. The food had just been prepared and was hot, right out of an oven! I looked up and down the street and there were no cars anywhere.

I took the food inside and placed the large kettle and pots on the stove. The kettle was full of pasta and meat and the pots had vegetables. Butter was also included with a loaf of fresh baked bread!

After dinner, we had a lot of food left over. My wife placed the leftover food in containers and we washed the kettle and pots and placed them on the small wooden steps. After about an hour, I checked on the kettle and pots and they were gone.

Later that same evening, my wife was prompted to ask the girls, "If you could have any kind of food, what would you want?" The girls, with their mother, prepared a list of the food they would like to have for the month. My wife and I also added to the list what we would like to eat.

4. This is a paraphrase of Stassen & Gushee, *Kingdom Ethics*, 453.

Sunday came and before my sermon, I shared how thankful our family was for the dinner someone had provided for us Friday evening. But no one knew about our need or who brought us dinner—No one gave even the slightest impression of knowing where the food had come from. Instead, they were just very thankful for God's faithfulness to their new pastor and his family!

I did not share that we had made lists of what we would like to have to eat in the coming month. But following our Sunday morning service, our church surprised us with a food shower. Every single item we had written on our lists was included among the food provided in the food shower!

I have been in the ministry for almost 40 years and God has never, never failed my family and me; in all his ways, God is faithful! Giving to the needs of others is always a great joy when you remember that everything you have, you received from God: *Every good and perfect gift is from above, coming down from the Father of the heavenly lights, who does not change like shifting shadows* (Ja. 1:17).

Living In The Way Of Jesus

Jesus leads us in a model prayer. "The Lord's Prayer" (6:9-15) begins with emphasis on the kingdom of heaven: *⁹ "This, then, is how you should pray: Our Father in heaven, hallowed be your name,' ¹⁰ your kingdom come, your will be done, on earth as it is in heaven."* Dallas Willard's words are inspiring: "Jesus' words and presence gave his followers faith to see that when he acted God also acted, that the governance or 'rule' of God came into play and thus was *at hand*. They were aware of the invisible presence of God acting within the visible reality and action of Jesus, the carpenter rabbi."[5]

Jesus' disciples are to pray for God's name to be hallowed, "holy, holy, holy, Lord God Almighty;" and we are to pray for the kingdom of God to come, and for God's will to "be done on earth as it is in heaven."

As we intensely pray for God's will on earth, we are asking for the kingdom of God "to take over at all points in the personal, social, and political order,"[6] where we "... see the wrong, the injustice, the violence and the sadness in the world's patterns and power arrangements."[7]

---

5. Willard, *The Divine Conspiracy*, 21.
6. Ibid., 26.
7. Stassen & Gushee, *Kingdom Ethics*, 460.

'When You Pray'

"The Lord's Prayer" is kingdom centered, that is, those who pray this prayer in faith, are willing to place the "kingdom of God and his righteousness" (Mt. 6:33) before all other hopes, dreams and pursuits in their personal lives. But as we seek first his kingdom and his righteousness, all these things will be given to us:[11] *"Give us today our daily bread.[12] And forgive us our debts, as we also have forgiven our debtors.[13] And lead us not into temptation, but deliver us from the evil one."*

Luther observed that "bread" (v. 11) represented "everything necessary for the preservation of this life, like food, a healthy body, good weather, house, home, wife, children, good government and peace."[8] In the same way "bread" is necessary for the sustaining of our physical life; and forgiveness (v. 12), both to be forgiven and to forgive "our debtors" is necessary for the sustaining of our soul ("debtors" is a good translation, for as God drops the charges against us, we are to drop the charges against those who are "indebted" to us because of their offense). And, "lead us not into temptation, but deliver us from the evil one" (v.13).

Spiritual Formation

1. What is the central theme of this chapter?
2. "The Lord's Prayer" is kingdom centered. . ." What does this mean and why is it so important to prayer?
3. What does Jesus mean by, "babbling like pagans"?
4. What are to be the motivations of our heart when we go to God in prayer?
5. What answers to prayer have profoundly changed the course of your life? [9]

---

8. Luther, *The Sermon on the Mount*, 147.

9. Mark Batterson's book, *The Circle Maker, Praying Circles Around Your Biggest Dreams and Greatest Fears* (Grand Rapids, MI.: Zondervan, 2011) is theologically solid, historically and biblically sound and extremely inspiring for personal and group study. This book will prove to be very beneficial for the prayer life of the believer!

Chapter 11

'When You Fast'

Matthew 6:16-18

Fasting is related to repentance and prayer for through the weakening of the flesh, our disciplined obedience will triumph over our inclination towards disobedience.

> **Mt. 6**—[16] "When you fast, do not look somber as the hypocrites do, for they disfigure their faces to show others they are fasting. Truly I tell you, they have received their reward in full. [17] But when you fast, put oil on your head and wash your face, [18] so that it will not be obvious to others that you are fasting, but only to your Father, who is unseen; and your Father, who sees what is done in secret, will reward you.

"*When you fast . . . .*" Fasting, as mentioned in chapter 9, "When You Give," is one of the three pillars of Jewish piety and therefore, it is assumed that disciples will fast.

But when you fast, "*. . . do not look somber as the hypocrites do . . .*"—the Greek term translated "somber" and "hypocrites" is a compound meaning: a "play actor" with a "sad, gloomy or sullen look."[1] The absence of anonymity (righteousness) results in a pretense of piety, "*. . . they disfigure their faces to show others . . . .*"

Chrysostom, the Archbishop of Constantinople and influential Church Father comments on how Christians in his day were so much like

---

1. BAGD, 845/758.

the hypocrites who, "*disfigure their faces*": "Some Christians compete with hypocrites in looking dismal while fasting. They do better to fast in secret."[2]

"*Truly I tell you, they have received their reward in full.*" The hypocrite desires that people see their "sacrificial spirituality" and may even be ashamed of their own undisciplined lives. This kind of "publicity," as opposed to anonymity, then becomes the hypocrite's empty reward.

"But When You Fast...Do Not ...As The Hypocrites Do"

To abstain from food is fasting. Since fasting necessarily involves faith and a desire to do God's will (Acts 13:2-3; 14:23), the definition of fasting may well extend to going without a meal, instead of all three meals and food (snacks) for a given day for a short time, or long time; fasting is a matter of faith and the leading of God's Spirit.

The Pharisees fasted twice a week, Mondays and Thursdays.[3] And John the Baptist's disciples regularly fasted, but Jesus' disciples did not. "*They said to him, 'John's disciples often fast and pray, and so do the disciples of the Pharisees, but yours go on eating and drinking.'*"[4] But here, in the Sermon on the Mount, Jesus expects his disciples to fast and he tells us how to fast.

Before the inauguration of his earthly ministry, Jesus fasted forty days and nights in the wilderness.[5] And in his response to the Pharisees and John's disciples, Jesus answered: "*How can the guests of the bridegroom mourn while he is with them? The time will come when the bridegroom will be taken from them; then they will fast.*"[6]

Biblically, fasting is related to self-denial and self-discipline. Fasting and humbling "ourselves before God" are biblical equivalents (Ps. 35:13; Is. 58:3;5).[7] The discipline of fasting is a necessary element of the Christian life. "Such customs have only one purpose—to make the disciples more

---

2. *Ancient Christian Commentary on Scripture, Matthew 1-13*, 140.
3. Luke 18:12, Stott, *The Message of the Sermon on the Mount*, 135.
4. Matthew 9:14/Luke 5:33.
5. Matthew 4:1-11/Luke 4:1-13.
6. Matthew 9:14.
7. Stott, *The Message of the Sermon on the Mount*, 136.

ready and cheerful to accomplish those things which God would have done."[8]

The spirit is willing when Jesus calls believers to "love your enemies," but the flesh is too strong; it prevents the spirit from being obedient. Fasting is related to repentance and prayer for through the weakening of the flesh; our disciplined obedience will then triumph over our inclination towards disobedience.

Prayer coupled with fasting weakens the strong grip of the flesh on our spirit (Ezra 8:23; Neh. 1:4; Lk. 2:37; Mk. 9:29; 1 Cor. 7:5), "When all is said and done, the life of faith is nothing if not an unending struggle of the spirit with every available weapon against the flesh. How is it possible to live the life of faith when we grow weary of prayer, when we lose our taste for reading the Bible, and when sleep, food and sensuality deprive us of the joy of communion with God?"[9]

Living In The Way Of Jesus

> **Mt. 6:** [17]*"But when you fast, put oil on your head and wash your face,* [18] *so that it will not be obvious to others that you are fasting, but only to your Father, who is unseen; and your Father, who sees what is done in secret, will reward you."*

"But," contrary to the hypocrites, *"when you fast;"* although penitent fasting sometimes involved a variety of forms of humiliation (e.g., self-affliction, neglecting personal hygiene, wearing dirty clothing) Jesus tells his disciples to clean and anoint themselves, trim your beards, and wash your face, in other words, conceal from others the fact that you are fasting.[10] And then, *"your Father, who sees what is done in secret, will reward you."*

---

8. Bonhoeffer, *The Cost of Discipleship*, 169.

9. Ibid., 171.

10. Keener notes that "penitent fasting included afflicting oneself (Lev. 23:32), for most Jewish people the most extreme fasts meant not only abstaining from food but also practicing other forms of self-abasement like not shaving, washing one's clothes, anointing or having intercourse," *Matthew*, 147.

'When You Fast'

Spiritual Formation

1. *What is the central theme of this chapter?*
2. *Why should believers fast?*
3. *How do you know if you are praying and fasting in accord with God's will?*
4. *What are some specific reasons for why you have fasted and what results have come from your fasting? How long should you fast?*
5. *How does fasting strengthen our resolve to be obedient to Christ?*
6. *Is fasting always abstaining from food and drink or can we fast in other ways, e.g., abstaining from T.V. for a month; or video games, sports, etc.?*

Chapter 12

'Treasures in Heaven'

Matthew 6:19-21

IF OUR POSSESSIONS ARE invested in God's reign of justice and mercy, then our hearts are also invested there.

> 6—[19] "Do not store up for yourselves treasures on earth, where moths and vermin destroy, and where thieves break in and steal. [20] But store up for yourselves treasures in heaven, where moths and vermin do not destroy, and where thieves do not break in and steal. [21] For where your treasure is, there your heart will be also. [22] "The eye is the lamp of the body. If your eyes are healthy, your whole body will be full of light. [23] But if your eyes are unhealthy, your whole body will be full of darkness. If then the light within you is darkness, how great is that darkness! [24] "No one can serve two masters. Either you will hate the one and love the other, or you will be devoted to the one and despise the other. You cannot serve both God and money.

Jesus places two treasures side by side: "treasures on earth" and "treasures in heaven." Since "treasures on earth" are subject to deterioration, corruption and theft and therefore are insecure and "treasures in heaven" are incorruptible and out of the reach of thieves and they are therefore secure, one's choice ought to be easy!

But given human nature, the choice is not so easy. Clarity concerning what Jesus is *not* saying will help our understanding. Stott points out that Scripture does not teach against the owning of possessions or private property.[1] As well, investing for the future or life insurance are not forbidden

---

1. Stott, *The Message of the Sermon on the Mount*, 154.

in Scripture. To the contrary, "Scripture praises the ant for storing in the summer the food it will need in the winter, and declares that the believer who makes no provision for his family is worse than an unbeliever."[2] And finally, we are to enjoy God's provision for us[3]: "So neither having possessions, nor making provision for the future, nor enjoying the gifts of a good Creator are included in the ban on earthly treasure-storage."[4]

But, the darkness of the human heart makes the choice between earthly treasures and heavenly treasures an excruciating one (c.f., Jer. 17:9). Matthew 6:19 asserts, [19] *"Do not store up for yourselves treasures on earth . . ."* literally reads: "Do not treasure up for yourselves treasures on earth." Stassen and Gushee point out that this is a "'play on words,' 'treasure up treasures,' connotes hoarding out of pride, greed and stinginess."[5]

Contrary to the heresy of the "health, wealth and prosperity" message still peddled by some "Tel-Evangelists," believers are not to pursue "treasures on earth." And whereas many believers rightly reject the "health, wealth, and prosperity" message, this does not mean that we are necessarily faithful stewards or generous givers.

The Bible requires us to give 10% of our income to "the storehouse," the local church, for the work of the ministry; for the church to "do justice," "love mercy" and "walk humbly" with God. But, even though Christians reportedly "take in 68 percent of the world's income, yet only 3 percent of that goes to the church and a tiny percentage to world missions."[6]

More precisely, the average Evangelical-Protestant Christian in America gives 2.6% of their income to the church; about 1/4 of what the Bible tells us to give. If believers in America gave 10% of their income to the cause of Christ—the tithe the Bible tells us to give—what could the remaining 7.4% accomplish? In 1 year, Evangelical Christians could eliminate extreme poverty worldwide; every child in the world could receive a primary education and health care for every person in need in the world could be provided for and there would still be 84 billion dollars left over.[7]

---

2. Ibid., 155; Proverbs. 6:6 ff.; 1 Tim. 5:8.
3. Ibid., 1 Tim. 4:3, 4; 6:17.
4. Ibid.
5. Stassen & Gushee, *Kingdom Ethics*, 410.
6. Keener, *Matthew*, 148-149.
7. Hurkman, *Venture Expeditions*, Sermon delivered at: Cedar Valley Assembly of God, January 13, 2013. For further information on this remarkable ministry, please see: "Venture: Events, Expeditions, Adventures," http://www.ventureexpeditions.org.

INSANITY!

A significant portion of the Evangelical-Protestant Church in America is ensnared by "pride, greed and stinginess" and consequently, they refuse to acknowledge the Lordship of Christ over their lives, they rather choose "treasures on earth."

Living In The Way Of Jesus

[20]*"But store up for yourselves treasures in heaven, where moths and vermin do not destroy, and where thieves do not break in and steal."* For Matthew, "heaven" is where God's glory and will are complete: *"To have one's treasure in heaven means to submit oneself totally to that which is in heaven—God's sovereign rule."*[8]

Bonhoeffer's insight is invaluable: "It is to be observed that Jesus does not deprive the human heart of its instinctive needs—treasure, glory and praise. But he gives it higher objects—the glory of God (John 5:44), the glorying in the cross (Gal. 6:14), and the treasure in heaven."[9] The believer is to invest his or her "treasures" in God's kingdom of justice, mercy and humble service (cf. Luke 4:18-19/Micah 6:8).

Verse 21: *"For where your treasure is, there your heart will be also"* is connected to verses 22-23: *"The eye is the lamp of the body. If your eyes are healthy, your whole body will be full of light,* [23] *But if your eyes are unhealthy, your whole body will be full of darkness. If then the light within you is darkness, how great is that darkness!"*

If our possessions are invested in God's reign of justice and mercy, then our hearts are also invested there.[10] And your "eyes are healthy." Jesus, in the Greek text, literally refers to the "eye" as "single."[11] To translate the Greek word "healthy" (as does the NIV) is to miss the Jewish significance of the term. The Greek version of the Hebrew Bible (known as the Septuagint and signified by the Roman numerals: LXX) uses the word literally meaning "single" as a translation of the Hebrew word for "perfect"—*Jesus is referring to a "single-minded" devotion to God; the believer's heart is set on God alone.*[12]

---

8. Stassen & Gushee, *Kingdom Ethics*, 410.
9. Bonhoeffer, *The Cost of Discipleship*, 176.
10. Stassen & Gushee, *Kingdom Ethics*, 411.
11. BAGD, 86.
12. Keener, *Matthew*, 150.

Contrarily, verse 23 literally reads: "But if the eye of you is evil;" the Greek word translated evil means, "in poor condition, sick."[13] The evil or bad eye cannot see properly; it is spiritually in a poor condition and sick because of its "hoarding out of pride, greed and stinginess." The next verse confronts the believer with a very weighty decision: [24] *"No one can serve two masters. Either you will hate the one and love the other, or you will be devoted to the one and despise the other. You cannot serve both God and money."* Literally, "You "are not able" to serve both God and wealth.[14] The gravitational pull of the heart will always draw a believer to prefer one master over the other—*If the eye of the believer "cannot see properly," that person will worry about holding onto their possessions.*

Spiritual Formation

1. *What is the central theme of this chapter?*
2. *What is the difference between giving because a believer can afford to give and giving in faith?*
3. *How can you tell if a person gives in faith instead of giving because they can afford to give?*
4. *Is a believer with a "single-eye" able to overcome worry if they decide to live a more modest life-style?*
5. *Do you know of believers who although they give generously they, never-the-less, worry about possessions and sustaining their wealth?*

---

13. BAGD, 690.
14. Stassen & Gushee, *Kingdom Ethics*, 412.

Chapter 13

'Do Not Worry'

Matthew 6:25-34

"Worry does not empty tomorrow of its sorrow, it empties today of its strength"

—Corry Ten-Boom.

[25] "Therefore I tell you, do not worry about your life, what you will eat or drink; or about your body, what you will wear. Is not life more than food, and the body more than clothes? [26] Look at the birds of the air; they do not sow or reap or store away in barns, and yet your heavenly Father feeds them. Are you not much more valuable than they? [27] Can any one of you by worrying add a single hour to your life?

[28] "And why do you worry about clothes? See how the flowers of the field grow. They do not labor or spin. [29] Yet I tell you that not even Solomon in all his splendor was dressed like one of these. [30] If that is how God clothes the grass of the field, which is here today and tomorrow is thrown into the fire, will he not much more clothe you— you of little faith? [31] So do not worry, saying, 'What shall we eat?' or 'What shall we drink?' or 'What shall we wear?' [32] For the pagans run after all these things, and your heavenly Father knows that you need them. [33] But seek first his kingdom and his righteousness, and all these things will be given to you as well. [34] Therefore do not worry about tomorrow, for tomorrow will worry about itself. Each day has enough trouble of its own."

'No One Can Serve Two Masters'

"*Therefore*" (6:25) is a conclusion drawn from the previous verse: [24] "*No one can serve two masters. Either you will hate the one and love the other, or you will be devoted to the one and despise the other. You cannot serve both God and money.*"

If you *"cannot see properly"* (6:23) because of covetousness, you will choose "treasures on earth" (money and possessions) over the Lordship of Christ in your life. And you will *therefore* obsessively worry (Greek: having anxiety; unduly concerned[1]) about holding onto your possessions. But if your eye is "single" (6:22), you will set your heart on God alone and you will be set free from worry.

Keener notes that Jesus "stresses that God guarantees only what we need. If God sustains life and protects our bodies, will we complain if he does it differently from the ways our culture values (v. 25). If he feeds us like the birds (v.26) or clothes us like the flowers (v.28), he will have provided us more than what our culture values, not less (v. 29)."[2]

Observe Jesus' use of a standard type of Jewish argument in stressing, "Are you not much more valuable" (v. 26) and "will he not much more" (v. 30). If God feeds the birds, though "they do not sow or reap or store away in barns," and "he clothes the flowers, apart from any need on their part to 'labor or spin,'" how much more will he care for his beloved children? A gentle reproof to "awaken persons all the more to the force of his words" follows, "*. . . you of little faith.*"[3]

Worry is incompatible with "living in the way of Jesus." God will provide all we need, [31] *So do not worry, saying, 'What shall we eat?' or 'What shall we drink?' or 'What shall we wear?'* But anxiety is compatible with paganism: [32]"*For the pagans run after all these things, and your heavenly Father knows that you need them.*"

Personal Peace & Social Affluence

Two prominent values: *personal peace* and *social affluence*, control the hearts of a majority in America, especially the middle class. The late Francis Schaeffer described these values this way:

1. BAGD, 505.
2. Keener, *Matthew*, 153.
3. Chrysostom, *The Gospel of Matthew*, "Homily," 22.1. *Matthew 1-13*, Oden, 145.

Personal Peace: "I want to be left alone; and I don't care what happens to the man across the street or across the world. I want my own lifestyle undisturbed, even regardless of what that will mean for my own children and grandchildren."

Affluence: "Things, things, things. Always more things, and success is seen as the abundance of things."[4] Social affluence, "has achieved nearly cultic status as a traditional American value."[5]

And consequently, Americans obsessively worry about holding onto their possessions. "Politics," observed Francis Schaeffer, "has largely become not a matter of ideals—increasingly men and women are not stirred by the values of liberty and truth—but of supplying a constituency with a frosting of personal peace and affluence. They know that voices will not be raised as long as people have these things, or at least an illusion of them."[6]

Would a significant portion of the American population, Christian and non-Christian alike, be inclined to uncritically accept the loss of liberties if our life-styles, driven by personal peace and affluence, were threatened?

Living In The Way Of Jesus

[33]*"But seek first his kingdom and his righteousness, and all these things will be given to you as well.* [34] *Therefore do not worry about tomorrow, for tomorrow will worry about itself. Each day has enough trouble of its own."*

Worry causes us to see life in distorted ways; it makes us vulnerable to thinking that life is something different from what it really is. Life begins to come into focus when we "look at the birds" and "see . . . the flowers." In the context of the Sermon on the Mount, Luther referred to the birds as "our schoolmasters and teachers" and Spurgeon spoke of how the flowers ". . . rebuke our foolish nervousness."[7] If God, our Father, cares for the birds and the flowers, why do we worry? *We worry, not because of our possessions or lack of them, we worry because we fail to focus on God.*

---

4. Elspeth, "The Age of Personal Peace and Affluence." See also: Schaeffer, "How Should We Then Live – 09. The Age of Personal Peace and Affluence."

5. Keener, *Matthew*, 151.

6. Schaeffer, *Complete Works*, Vol. 5, *How Should We Then Live?* 227.

7. Stott, *The Message of the Sermon on the Mount*, 164-165.

If we strive to walk in God's will, if we turn ourselves over to the all-consuming presence of God, we are assured of God's provision (6:33). In the "Lord's Prayer" (Mt. 6:9-10), Jesus' disciples are told to seek first God's kingdom. Faith is not a means to move God to give us what we want, "faith is obeying God's will with the assurance that he will ultimately fulfill for us what is in our best interests."[8]

"Can any one of you by worrying add a single hour to your life?" Worry *"about tomorrow"* is not in our best interests; rather than adding to the length of our lives, worry shortens our lives, it diminishes our strength and creates ill-affects upon our health.

All we need comes from God. By means of our generosity towards others, we become intimately involved in God's providential purposes in the earth: "Therefore, we can hardly live under God's reign, receive his blessings, and not use them to help alleviate the evil of hunger and need elsewhere . . . . Not only do we recognize that all we have comes from God, but we also recognize that sharing that with others to remove their suffering is to defeat the enemy and to 'seek the Kingdom . . . on earth as in heaven.'"[9] We will overcome worry if we are generous towards those in need in the same way God has been so generous to us; *"acting justly" towards the needy frees us to seek first God's kingdom and his righteousness.*

Spiritual Formation

1. *What is the central theme of this chapter?*
2. *When Jesus tells us, "do not worry" what is he specifically referring to? How do we overcome worry?*
3. *Is it wrong to worry about the health or welfare of a loved one?*
4. *Does faith or prayer move God, or do they place us in God's will for our lives?*
5. *How do you understand and relate to the "sovereignty of God?"*

---

8. Keener, *Matthew*, 154.

9. Guelich, *The Sermon on the Mount: A Foundation for Understanding*, 373. In: Stassen & Gushee, *Kingdom Ethics*, 41.

Chapter 14

Judging Others

Matthew 7:1-6; 12

"If there is no absolute by which to judge society, society is absolute"

—Francis Schaeffer.

7— *"Do not judge, or you too will be judged.* ² *For in the same way you judge others, you will be judged, and with the measure you use, it will be measured to you.*

³ *"Why do you look at the speck of sawdust in your brother's eye and pay no attention to the plank in your own eye?* ⁴ *How can you say to your brother, 'Let me take the speck out of your eye,' when all the time there is a plank in your own eye?* ⁵ *You hypocrite, first take the plank out of your own eye and then you will see clearly to remove the speck from your brother's eye.*

⁶ *"Do not give dogs what is sacred; do not throw your pearls to pigs. If you do, they may trample them under their feet, and turn and tear you to pieces.*

Mt. 7:1—*"Do not judge. . .."* The word translated "judge" means: "pass judgment upon;"[1] to use "sharp, unjust criticism"[2]... *"or you too will be judged."* That is, you will be judged (placed on trial) by the divine tribunal[3]—"Do

1. BAGD, 452.
2. Robertson, Vol. I., 60.
3. BAGD, 452.

Judging Others

not harshly condemn others or you will be judged by God." Verse 2: *"For in the same way you judge others, you will be judged. . ."*—You will be judged by the same criteria and capacity of criticism you apply in judging others.[4]

In verses 3-4, Jesus focuses on the "measure" we use to judge others. Several years ago, I read a piercing illustration in Francis Schaeffer's, *The Church at the End of the Twentieth Century*:

> Imagine that each baby is born into the world with an invisible tape recorder hung around his neck. Imagine further that these are very special recorders that record only when moral judgments are made. Aesthetic judgments such as "This is beautiful" are not recorded. But whenever a person makes such a statement as "She's such a gossip," or "He's so lazy," the recorder turns on, records the statement and turns off.
>
> Many times each day the recorder operates, as the person makes moral judgments about those around him, recording dozens of judgments each week, hundreds every year and thousands in a lifetime.
>
> Then the scene shifts, and we suddenly see all the people of the world standing before God at the end of time. "God, it's not fair for You to judge me," say some. "I didn't know about Christ." "No one taught me the Ten Commandments, and I never read the Sermon on the Mount."
>
> Then God speaks. "Very well. Since you claim not to know My laws, I will set aside My perfect standard of righteousness. Instead I will judge you on this." And as He pushes the button on the recorder, the person listens with growing horror as his own voice pours forth a stream of condemnation toward those around him . . . "She shouldn't be doing this." "He was wrong in that," thousands upon thousands of moral judgments.
>
> When the tape ends, God says, "This will be the basis of My judgment: how well have you kept the moral standards you proved that you understood by constantly applying them to those around you. Here you accused someone of lying, yet have you ever stretched the truth? You were angry at that fellow for being selfish, yet have you ever put your own interests above someone else's needs?" And every person will be silent. For no one has consistently lived up to the standard he demands of others.[5]

---

4. Ibid., 515.
5. Schaeffer, *The Church at the End of the Twentieth Century*, pp. 49-50.

INSANITY!

Before we too harshly judge another, we need to consider our own criterion for morality and ethics. And then decide, based on our own criterion, if we flawlessly live up to the "measure" we use to judge another. The "speck" and "plank" metaphors will then become painfully self-evident.[6]

Jesus concludes his thought:

> Mt. 7—[6] *"Do not give dogs what is sacred; do not throw your pearls to pigs. If you do, they may trample them under their feet, and turn and tear you to pieces."* In view of Jesus' warning, Paul provides resolve: *"Therefore judge nothing before the appointed time; wait till the Lord comes. He will bring to light what is hidden in darkness and will expose the motives of men's hearts. At that time each will receive his praise from God"* (cf.,1 Cor. 4:5).

While we wait for the Lord's return, Stassen and Gushee wisely counsel us to take responsibility for our biases: "Our own bias in perceiving and misperceiving our social situation are caused by our misplaced loyalties to other lords in our lives besides God (Mt. 6:21-23), and by our self-righteous judgmentalism."[7]

Political Correctness: Justice And Injustice Look The Same

A very perceptive journalist recently observed: "America, the country, is as divided as it has been in 150 years, since the Civil War. Right and Left live in entirely different cultures in a lot of ways, rarely encountering one another personally. They live in different cities, attend different churches, read different books, even have different hobbies; they even eat different foods increasingly.

At the political level, state and local governments don't just denounce federal policy, they actively defy it. Eight states defy the federal ban on marijuana letting citizens grow and sell it with impunity.

Countless cities tell their police to pretend immigration laws don't exist or are invalid or so immoral you can ignore them. Can we salvage a

---

6. Davies and Allen, *Exegetical Commentary on the Gospel According to St. Matthew*, Vol. 1, 673, elegantly assert: "Human beings unhappily possess an inbred proclivity to mix ignorance of themselves with arrogance toward others."

7. Stassen & Gushee, *Kingdom Ethics*, 178.

functional nation out of two groups who increasingly despise each other? It's a real question and not asked often enough."[8]

"Right and Left live in entirely different cultures in a lot of ways, rarely encountering one another personally," consequently most Americans think that any attempt at having a normal conversation with a person different from themselves would be so difficult or uncomfortable, we rather choose to avoid one another.

Evangelical Christians consistently admit that they have significant problems communicating with people not like themselves. For example, nearly 9 in 10 Evangelical Christians (87%) report higher tensions than any other group in American culture when it comes to normal conversation with an LGBTQ person or a Muslim.[9] Further, 85% of Evangelicals have increased anxiety when it comes to dialogue with atheists or people unaffiliated with any other faith.[10] Perhaps even more surprisingly, nearly 3 in 10 Evangelicals, nearly 1/3 (28%), report having difficulty engaging in normal conversation with other Evangelicals.[11]

Compared to Evangelicals, a much lower percentage of LGBTQ people (58%) say they have difficulty sharing in a normal conversation with a Christian.[12] 69% of people in faiths other than Christian report that a conversation with an Evangelical Christian is difficult for them while 55% of U.S. adults in general admit that they have problems talking with [Evangelical/born-again] Christians.[13] Our problems associating with one another, especially people different from ourselves, doesn't appear to be helped by social media.

As our culture increasingly becomes more like Europe, that is, increasingly secularized ("post-Christian"), Christian morality is fast-fading from American life. As the moral vacuum grows in America, many U.S. adults are admitting that they are uncertain about how to differentiate right from wrong.[14]

A majority among American adults, 57%, of our nations' population to include all ages, ethnicities, genders, socioeconomic categories and

---

8. "Tucker Carlson Tonight," Fox News, 04/27/2017, 8:00 P.M., EST.
9. *Barna Trends, 2017,* "Americans Struggle to Talk Across Divides," 115.
10. Ibid.
11. Ibid.
12. Ibid.
13. Ibid.
14. Ibid., "The New Moral Code," 50.

political ideological views, believe "knowing what is right or wrong is a matter of personal experience."[15]

Differentiating between good and bad, moral and immoral, is now a purely subjective choice. America's majority moral code has become: "The morality of self-fulfillment" and now, the highest good in our society involves "finding yourself" and then living by "what's right for you."[16]

Statistics related to the "morality of self-fulfillment" and responses from "all U.S. Adults" and "practicing Christians"—"practicing Christians," as distinguished from Evangelical and/or born-again Christians, are described as "self-identified Christians who say their faith is very important in their lives and have attended a worship service within the past month"[17]—are morally troubling.

For example, in response to the statement: "The best way to find yourself is by looking within yourself," 91% of U.S. adults "completely" or "somewhat" agreed compared to 76% of practicing Christians. In response to the assertion: "People should not criticize someone else's life choices," 89% of U.S. adults "completely" or "somewhat" agreed compared to 76% of practicing Christians and to the notion: "Any kind of sexual expression between two consenting adults is acceptable," 69% of U.S. adults "completely" or "somewhat" agreed compared to 40% of practicing Christians.[18]

But when the "morality of self-fulfillment" is on display in our culture, especially in high profile ways, it generates considerably more confusion than moral clarity. Consider, for example, the stories of three people: Elizabeth Warren, Rachel Dolezal and Caitlyn Jenner. Two of these women, Warren and Dolezal, assumed racial identities different from their original race at birth and Jenner chose sexual reassignment.

Rachel Dolezal was formerly the head of the Spokane, Washington NAACP but she was forced to resign because it was "discovered" that she is not black. She is the daughter of white parents and she was born and raised in Montana as a freckle-faced strawberry blond. Rachel was socially charged with "cultural appropriation." Cultural appropriation is a charge made against people who have allegedly hijacked elements common to one culture and applied them to a different culture.

---

15. Ibid.
16. Ibid., 53.
17. This definition of "practicing Christians" is used by Barna researchers, Ibid.,10.
18. Ibid., 53.

In her defense against the charge of "cultural appropriation," Rachel Dolezal has tirelessly contended that race is simply a "social construct" and she is "transracial." But her defense has fallen on deaf ears and she has instead been widely ridiculed, slandered and abused.

Caitlyn Jenner has, however, been celebrated and consistently referred to as "brave" and "courageous" for identifying as "transsexual." ESPN bestowed the "Arthur Ash Courage Award" on Caitlyn Jenner in 2015. And later, in the same year, Caitlyn was named Glamour Magazine's "Woman of the Year."

Why does "cultural appropriation" provoke hostility but sexual reassignment or "biological appropriation" is celebrated? How is individual expression in an outward biological form of how one feels on the inside, different from racial expression on the outside of how one feels on the inside? So, biology can be appropriated, but cultural/ racial identity cannot be?

In his article, "Rachel Dolezal is Every Bit as Black as Caitlyn Jenner is Female," Dan Foley asks the daring, but obvious question: "Can you imagine anyone confronting Caitlyn with pictures of herself as a young Bruce Jenner, as though such pictures could prove that Caitlyn is not a woman?"[19] Foley's question is, of course, rhetorical.

However, when you think about it, was ESPN guilty of a "microaggression"? (A microaggression is a common term used on university campuses for a small action or choice of words that although on their face pose no malicious intent but subtly represent a kind of violence nonetheless).[20]

In other words, when ESPN honored Caitlyn Jenner with the "Arthur Ash Courage Award," why else was she standing in front of a room full of great athletes unless she herself had been one "in a previous biological life?" Could ESPN's insensitivity have been, at least in the understanding of millennials at preeminent universities such as Yale, a "trigger"[21] for a traumatic recurrence of Jenner's struggles that perhaps had eventually led to her sexual reassignment?

Since political correctness does not allow for moral reasoning to be founded on objective criteria, what can we conclude regarding ESPN's apparent insensitivity? Perhaps, and I am speculating, since "cultural appropriation" is an apparent violation of the "cultural rights" of an entire culture, but sexual reassignment or biological appropriation evidently offends no

---

19. Foley, "Rachel Dolezal is Every Bit as Black as Caitlyn Jenner is Female."
20. Lukianoff and Haidt, *The Atlantic*, September 2015.
21. Ibid.

INSANITY!

one, or at least only an intolerant family member or two, then it is to be "tolerated"? But I am confused. If Dolezal and Jenner are autonomous persons and therefore, their personal moral choices are purely subjective, why are they treated differently? For that matter, why does anyone have the right to be outraged by another person's moral choices?

And further, if Rachel Dolezal was guilty of some egregious social transgression punishable by slander, abuse and ridicule, followed by her resignation as the head of the Spokane, Washington NAACP in disgrace, then what about Elizabeth Warren?

Prior to becoming a tenured member of the Harvard Law School faculty in the mid-1990's, Senator Warren claimed Cherokee and Delaware Indian ancestry. But, Garance Franke-Ruta observes otherwise, "Elizabeth Warren is not a citizen of the Cherokee Nation. Elizabeth Warren is not enrolled in the Eastern Band of Cherokee Indians. And Elizabeth Warren is not one of the United Keetoowah Band of Cherokee."[22]

According to independent genealogists, Warren's claim to having even 1/32 Cherokee ancestry is unsubstantiated; Senator Warren is not eligible to become a recognized member of the Cherokee Nation.[23] Why has Rachel Dolezal been disgraced but Elizabeth Warren continues to rise in power as a probable presidential candidate for the Democratic Party in 2020? Should not Warren resign her Senate seat in disgrace?

Our culture is consistently inconsistent. Caught up in a vicious cycle of insanity, our quest for an absolute unbridled (autonomous) freedom, that is, freedom without any restraints, without any form or outside Transcendent or Absolute to guide us will inevitably lead us "in the direction of an establishment totalitarianism."[24] *"If there is no absolute by which to judge society, society is absolute."*[25]

---

22. Franke-Ruta, "Is Elizabeth Warren Native American or What?"
23. Ibid.
24. Schaeffer, "The Church at the End of the Twentieth Century," 25.
25. Wilson observes that If race "is a social construct," . . . "that means there is no such thing as racism. Right? Sex is also entirely a matter of what you believe deep down in your heart, chromosomes be damned, and so it necessarily follows that there is no such thing as sexism," "Southern Baptist Lava Lamps."

JUDGING OTHERS

Living In The Way Of Jesus

7—¹² *So in everything, do to others what you would have them do to you, for this sums up the Law and the Prophets.*

William Wilberforce (1759-1833) was a principled politician, a Christian statesman whose uncompromising convictions enabled him to transcend party lines for the sake of the common good of society.[26] In his cultural apologetic, *A Practical View of Christianity*, Wilberforce writes, "If indeed through the blessing of Providence, a principle of true Religion should in any considerable degree gain ground, there is no estimating the effects on public morals, and the consequent influence on our political welfare."[27]

Wilberforce and his Anglican Christian community, the Clapham Group, are an inspiring historic picture of how: (1) social reform is an essential part of people's willingness to hear the gospel; (2) the Spirit-filled life is not about withdrawing from the culture, but, believers immersing themselves in it and transforming it from within; (3) the local church can transform culture by inspiring believers to take social and political responsibility seriously as an essential part of sharing the gospel of Jesus Christ; and (4) Wilberforce and the Clapham Sect's grassroots political philosophy effectively forced the British Parliament to support their moral-ethical reforms.

Inspired by the "Golden Rule," William Wilberforce, "the conscience of the nation," contended: "If any country were indeed filled with men, each thus diligently discharging the duties of his own station without breaking in upon the rights of others, but on the contrary endeavoring, so far as he might be able, to forward their views and promote their happiness, all would be active and harmonious in the goodly frame of human society."[28] The four pillars of Wilberforce's political philosophy are set forth in this quote: conscientious stewardship; respect for the rights of others; advancing the views of others and the promotion of the happiness of others.

Regarding stewardship, Wilberforce stressed that every person is endowed by God with "means and occasions . . . of improving ourselves, or

---

26. William Wilberforce is most known for the abolishing of slavery, first in the British Colonies and then in Great Britain itself; Wilberforce inspired Abraham Lincoln. See Belmonte, *William Wilberforce. A Hero for Humanity* (Grand Rapids, MI: Zondervan, 2007) for the best of numerous books on "the friend of Africa," William Wilberforce.

27. Wilberforce, *A Practical View of Christianity*, 229.

28. Ibid., 221.

INSANITY!

of promoting the happiness of others."[29] The conscientious stewardship of God's blessings upon individuals is to be used for the common good of society. This is a sacred duty for all people, especially Christians.

The grounds for every philanthropic and human rights issue is the Golden Rule in Wilberforce's political philosophy. The second political pillar, therefore, the respect for the rights of others, requires "everyone to regulate his conduct by the golden rule of doing to others as in similar circumstances we would have them do to us; and the path of duty will be clear before him, and I will add, the decision of [a] legislature would scarcely any longer be doubtful."[30]

Promoting the views of others, the third of Wilberforce's political ideals, involves the practical application of the Golden Rule: place the views of others before the self, that is, hear with understanding what is in the hearts of other people.

Wilberforce's fourth political strategy is the promotion of the happiness of others. Whereas Jefferson's ideal was the personal "pursuit of happiness," Wilberforce believed it was better to promote the happiness of others, surely this serves to promote one's own happiness in fuller, more meaningful ways.

In 1787, two years after his conversion to Christianity, Wilberforce's political philosophy, the Golden Rule, in the context of the Sermon on the Mount, began taking narrative form in his life as he penned the concentration of his deepest convictions: "God Almighty has set before me two great objects: the suppression of the slave trade and the reformation of manners."

On February 23, 1807, following twenty years of unrelenting criticism, threats on his life, stubborn prejudice on the part of his colleagues in Parliament, and a serious illness in 1788 that almost claimed Wilberforce's life, a Bill for the Abolition of the Slave Trade was passed in the House by a vote of 283 to 16.[31]

After another twenty-six years of enduring political, social, and spiritual battles the Emancipation Bill abolishing slavery in all the British colonies passed in Parliament on July 26, 1833. Three days later, following forty-six years of steadfast faith in the face of overwhelming odds, Wilberforce died.

---

29. Belmonte, *William Wilberforce*, 177.
30. Ibid.
31. Vaughan, *Statesman and Saint: The Principled Politics of William Wilberforce*, 93.

Wilberforce's "Vital Christianity" is committed to the common good of culture by its unashamed, single-minded commitment to the Cross, and the dynamic power of the Holy Spirit's presence in the lives of believers.[32] Wilberforce and his Christian community, the Clapham Group, related their understanding of a "Vital Christianity" to the deepest longings of British culture and consequently, they laid the foundations for the Victorian era in the next generation, an age of manners and of civility.

Spiritual Formation

1. *What is the central theme of this chapter?*

2. *Why are Evangelical born-again Christians so uncomfortable dialoguing with people different from themselves?*

3. *How is Wilberforce's application of the Golden Rule radically contrary to politically correct "Tolerance"?*

4. *How did Wilberforce avoid looking pass the plank in his own eye while pointing out the speck in the eye of an adversary to his Christian faith?*

---

32. Vital Christianity ought not to be confused with liberal Christianity's "social gospel." The social gospel equates the kingdom of God with social revitalization, Wilberforce clearly believed that the displacing of the Cross with social revitalization as the end of the Gospel was anathema.

Chapter 15

'Enter Through the Narrow Gate'

Matthew 7:13-14; 21-23

"I am the way and the truth and the life. No one comes to the Father except through me"—Jesus Christ

7—[13] *"Enter through the narrow gate. For wide is the gate and broad is the road that leads to destruction, and many enter through it.* [14] *But small is the gate and narrow the road that leads to life, and only a few find it.*

THE NARROW GATE IS not doctrinal correctness but rather, it's obedience. But who requires our obedience? Jesus himself is "the narrow way and the strait gate. He, and he alone, is our journey's end. When we know that, we are able to proceed along the narrow way through the strait gate of the cross, and onto eternal life, and the very narrowness of the road will increase our certainty."[1]

The broad gate is simply interpreting life, and specifically the way of Jesus, by means of contemporary norms and prevailing cultural trends. In this case, religious pluralism is the "broad gate." Their clothing appears to be "enlightened, and up-to-date" but inwardly, they have great contempt towards Christ because of the narrow way to life He offers.

---

1. Bonhoeffer, *The Cost of Discipleship*, 191.

'Enter Through the Narrow Gate'
Religious Pluralism: A Wide Gate And Broad Road

In the thinking of religious pluralists, the various religions of the world all derive from a common genus: "the lamps are different, but the Light is the same."[2] The "Real" (i.e., the common genus of all religions) is ineffable: "the sacred is a mystery beyond all our concepts and images" and therefore, "no vision can adequately represent God."[3]

How is the ineffable "Real" related to the religions of the world? John Hick explains:

> Well, if religion is a response, or a range of responses, what is it a response to? Christianity says the Holy Trinity; Islam, the strictly unitary Allah; Hinduism says that it is Brahman; and so on. But in regarding each of these, and the other major world traditions, as more or less equally effective contexts of salvation/liberation, we are regarding them as responses to that to which religion is a response—which I am referring to as the Real.[4]

Religious pluralism's "inclusiveness" insists that all the world's religions are equal contexts for "salvation" or "liberation;" all humanity will ultimately partake of God's salvation. And consequently, religious pluralists are opposed to "exclusivism," particularly, "Christian exclusivism."

Christian exclusivism—*"Salvation is found in no one else for there is no other name [Jesus Christ] under heaven given to men by which we must be saved"*—is considered intolerable by pluralists because it can no longer be considered *intellectually honest* or *morally acceptable* in the context of contemporary knowledge of other world religions and faiths. And thus, religious pluralists level two types of objections against "religious exclusivism": *moral* and *intellectual*.

---

2. *Rami: Poet and Mystic,* Nicholson, 166. In, Hick, *A Christian Theology of Religions*, 37.

3. Reeves, "God at 2000," *Gazette-Times*, Corvallis, Oregon, February 12, 2000, A7.

4. Hick, *A Christian Theology of Religions*, 67. Harvard's Diana Eck opines: "In matters of religion there is no simultaneous translation by which I say "God," and in the earphones of others it becomes 'Allah,' 'Vishnu,' 'Kali,' or 'Amitabha.' These are not the same, nor are they totally different. Each is an entry point into a complex way of envisioning reality. Each contains within itself a multitude of names and attributes: the ninety-nine beautiful names of Allah, the thousand names of Vishnu, or the thousand names of Kali. As a Christian and as a scholar of the history of religions, I use the English word *God* so commonly and in so many different ways," "Honest to God," *God At 2000*, Edited by: Marcus Borg & Ross Mackenzie (Harrisburg, PA: Morehouse Publishing, 2000), 25.

INSANITY!

Moral Objections To "Religious Exclusivism"

If the exclusivist believes that: (1) *the Holy Spirit's internal witness to saving faith in Christ is assurance of personal salvation* and (2) *apart from a person having the Spirit, they do not belong to Christ*, then he or she must logically believe that those who hold to something incompatible with these evangelical premises have embraced error.

Religious pluralists charge that this view is *intolerable* in the context of contemporary knowledge of other religions and faiths. But is this charge against "exclusivists" justified?[5]

Only on an extremely theoretical level of speculation can the religious pluralist delude himself into believing that the laws of logic do not apply to his "open," "inclusive" or "pluralistic" point of view. For religious pluralism to be an acceptable option either: (1) there is no "God;" or (2) if there is a "God," he she or it does not hold people accountable for what they believe or how they live their lives. But such a god is profoundly unique from all other conceptions of the divine in any of the world's major religions.

Further, religious pluralism's profoundly unique conception of "god" (the "common genus") is placed above all other conceptions of the divine in the thinking of pluralists. And consequently, religious pluralists promote their own brand of exclusivism—*religious pluralists are guilty of the very thing for which they condemn exclusivists.*[6]

Among thinking individuals, discrimination between competing views is both acknowledged and practiced, and therefore, "exclusivism" is, logically speaking, unavoidable. Ironically, John Hick, a religious pluralist (quoted above), agrees with the implications of this conclusion: "To say that whatever is sincerely believed and practiced is, by definition, true, would be the end of all critical discrimination, both intellectual and moral."[7]

Ravi Zacharias further comments on the fallacy of religious pluralism: "To deem all beliefs equally true is sheer nonsense for the simple reason

---

5. The pluralist considers the "exclusivist" to be arrogant, triumphal, imperialistic and dishonest. The allegations of the pluralist against the exclusivist are, for the most part, *ad hominem*. The *ad hominem* fallacy occurs when a person (in this case, the exclusivist) is the focus of attack instead of his position.

6. My argument is a paraphrase of Tim Keller's apologetic. See, Tim Keller, "There Can't Be Just *One* True Religion," *The Reason for God, Belief in an Age of Skepticism*, 3-21.

7. Hick, *Truth and Dialogue*, 148.

that to deny that statement would also, then be true. But if the denial of the statement is also true, then all religions are not true."[8]

Intellectual Objections To "Exclusivism"

Religious pluralists charge that exclusivists are thinking in an intellectually arbitrary manner regarding their acceptance of the two exclusivist premises: (1) *The Holy Spirit's internal witness to saving faith in Christ is assurance of personal salvation* and (2) *apart from a person having the Spirit, they do not belong to Christ.*[9]

Nicholas Kristof, Columnist for the *New York Times*, concisely states the perceived problem: "I'm troubled by the evangelical notion that people go to heaven only if they have a direct relationship with Jesus. Doesn't that imply that billions of people—Buddhists, Jews, Muslims, Hindus—are consigned to hell because they grew up in non-Christian families around the world? That Gandhi is in hell?"[10]

What should we conclude from the observations of the religious pluralists? Does the truth of an individual's religion depend on their place of birth, the time of their birth or the ideological or religious orientation they were induced to accept during childhood?

More to the point, what may be wrong with believing that Gandhi should be saved apart from faith in Christ? The implication regarding Gandhi, admittedly, an example of a life well lived, is that people would be approaching God on grounds of their own goodness. "This would," observes Tim Keller, "ironically, actually be *more* exclusive and unfair, since so often those that we tend to think of as 'bad'—the abusers, the haters, the feckless and selfish—have themselves often had abusive and brutal backgrounds."[11] Christians believe that those who acknowledge and admit their weakness and need for a Savior receive salvation; access to God is freely offered to *anyone* through the grace of Jesus and eternal life then becomes their destiny instantly.[12]

The Cross is evidence that God cares about injustice and evil. Christian faith simply requires that *all* people acknowledge that because of their

---

8. Zacharias, *Jesus Among Other Gods*, 4.
9. Romans 8:9-11.
10. Kristof, *New York Times*, "Am I a Christian, Pastor Timothy Keller?"
11. Ibid.
12. Paraphrase of Keller's view, Ibid.

own sin—their willful unconformity to God's will for their life—they are incapable of *satisfying* God's ultimate justice.

Religious pluralism, in conclusion, is "beguiled by the cosmetically courteous idea that sincerity or privilege of birth is all that counts and that truth is subject to the beholder. In no other discipline of life can one be so naive as to claim inherited belief or insistent belief as the sole determiner of truth. Why, then, do we make the catastrophic error of thinking that all religions are right and that it does not matter whether the claims they make are objectively true?"[13]

Living In The Way Of Jesus

> Mt. 7—[21] "Not everyone who says to me, 'Lord, Lord,' will enter the kingdom of heaven, but only he who does the will of my Father who is in heaven. [22] Many will say to me on that day, 'Lord, Lord, did we not prophesy in your name, and in your name drive out demons and perform many miracles?' [23] Then I will tell them plainly, 'I never knew you. Away from me, you evildoers!'"

Many people claim to know Jesus Christ, but only those who obediently do the will of the Father will enter His kingdom: *"For my Father's will is that everyone who looks to the Son and believes in him shall have eternal life, and I will raise him up at the last day"* (Jn. 6:40). Jesus Christ *alone*, is able to save: *"Salvation is found in no one else, for there is no other name under heaven given to men by which we must be saved,"* (Acts 4:12).

But what if they "prophesied in his name"; and "in his name drove out demons" and "performed miracles"? There is no shortage of counterfeit miracles, signs and wonders among the deceived trapped in cults, and entangled in the occult (cf. 2 Thess. 2:9).

But true Biblical miracles are unique events, taking place within history, having moral value (*"Now to each one the manifestation of the Spirit is given for the common good,"* 1 Cor. 12:7) and requiring a theological explanation (". . .the same Spirit;" ". . . the same Lord;" and ". . . the same God" are "at work" in demonstrating divine power in the church, 1 Cor. 12:4-6). A Biblical miracle points to its source, the living God, whereas occult phenomenon is non-evidential and amoral, pointing to the individual performing the alleged supernatural act.

---

13. Zacharias, *Jesus Among Other Gods*, 7.

'Enter Through the Narrow Gate'

In the case of the New Testament, miracles are factually presented, in plain, intelligible terms and as having publicly taken place, that is, biblical miracles are open to testing and verification (1 Thess. 5:21-22).

The messianic credentials of Jesus of Nazareth are attested to by eyewitnesses of His power to heal: "The blind receive their sight, and the lame walk, the lepers are cleansed and the deaf hear, the dead are raised" (Mt. 11:5). And on the last day, the risen Christ will raise up those who believe in Him and they will enter through the "small gate" and "narrow road."[14] All others will be turned away—*"Then I will tell them plainly, 'I never knew you. Away from me, you evildoers!'"*[15]

Spiritual Formation

1. *What is the central theme of this chapter?*
2. *Why is exclusivism unavoidable?*
3. *How is the "finished work" of Christ both inclusive and exclusive?*
4. *Why can't any person "satisfy" God's justice on their own?*

---

14. For reasoned defense of the historical resurrection of Jesus Christ, please see my: *A Letter From Christ, Apologetics in Cultural Transition,* "The 'Sign of Jonah': Beyond Reasonable Doubt?"

15. This word translated "evildoers" is a term meaning: "lawless deeds," "transgressions," BAGD, 72.

Chapter 16

A Wise Builder

Matthew 7:24-27

"Where do I go for answers to life's most important questions?" And, "Is my source reliable?"—Harold Lindsell

Mt. 7—[24] *"Therefore everyone who hears these words of mine and puts them into practice is like a wise man who built his house on the rock."* [25] *The rain came down, the streams rose, and the winds blew and beat against that house; yet it did not fall, because it had its foundation on the rock.* [26] *But everyone who hears these words of mine and does not put them into practice is like a foolish man who built his house on sand.* [27] *The rain came down, the streams rose, and the winds blew and beat against that house, and it fell with a great crash."*

"Everyone Who Hears These Words..."

PROGRESSIVE SECULARIST ANGER NOW dominates the pubic square, to include numerous university campuses nation-wide. A common charge among progressives against the Christian faith is: *"Since the Bible is an ancient, unchanging book, it is outdated and obsolete. The Bible is therefore incapable of providing solutions for the staggering moral-ethical complexities of the twenty-first century!"*

During a Spring evening at the La Salle Stewart Center on the Oregon State University campus, following Dominic Crossan's discussion of the Bible, and other ancient spiritual writings (e.g., The Gospel of Thomas,

A Wise Builder

The Kabbalah and The Urantia), a gentleman asked the progressive Roman Catholic New Testament scholar: "When is the Bible going to be updated and made relevant for present-day needs?"

Tim Keller responds to this type of question by pointing out the assumption that lies behind it: Those who charge that the Bible has been outdated since at least the Dark Ages usually assume their place in history is the ultimate, climatic point in human history, but it's not.[1] Keller continues to explain that critiques of the Bible, made in every age, pass with every age; they end up in the "dust bin of history within a generation of time!" But orthodox Christianity remains the same.

For example, Augustine's *City of God* was written over 1,500 years ago. Augustine was defending the Christian faith against the cultural critiques of his day. A profound problem surfaces: When a person attempts to read Augustine's *City of God*, they find it to be very challenging to read. Why? Because although the skeptics of Augustine's day were all weighing in with their criticisms of the Bible and Christian faith, they are now so obsolete (even silly) that no one takes them seriously! But Augustine's defense of historic Christianity remains the same; and the historic Christian faith is still embraced by literally billions of people.

Keller acutely observes that 100 years from now, when the present-day critiques of Christian faith have passed, and been forgotten, orthodox Christianity will continue to remain the same. If you want to be up-to-date in every age, embrace orthodox Christianity and the living Word upon which it is founded!

And therefore, Keller concludes: If you accept the authority of the Bible, you are embracing an enduring city and therefore, your beliefs will never be out-of-date[2]—*You will be "like a wise man who built his house on the rock"!*

---

1. This is a typical secular progressive charge.

2. Keller, "The City to Come," Hebrews 11:13-16; 13:10-16, Copy-Write Redeemer Presbyterian Church, New York, NY. (Re: Contact for clarification in documenting Keller's work: Clara Lee, Project Manager, Redeemer City to City, NY, NY 1001).

INSANITY!

7—24 ". . . And Puts Them Into Practice. . ."

God's covenant people are ". . . declaring that something that wasn't previously the case is now going to be; that the life of heaven, which had seemed so distant and unreal, is in the process of coming true on earth."[3]

Living In The Way Of Jesus

The Sermon On The Mount Taking Narrative Form In Believer's Lives

The kingdom of God is not merely an abstract idea but present reality for God's covenant people. A disciple of Jesus Christ possesses a "unique understanding of the time of the End"—A disciple sees the present kingdom as the first-fruits of the future kingdom. This paradox reality—this "unique understanding of the time of the End"—results in the disciple seeing "an underlying continuity between present bodily life and future bodily life, and that gives meaning and direction to present Christian living"[4]—*Our daily lives are conditioned by both our connection to Jesus' historical resurrection and our future imperishable, immortal and incorruptible resurrection and that is the source of ultimate meaning for every ordinary day of our lives* (*cf.* Rom. 4:25/1 Cor. 15:42-58).

The Spirit empowered believer's unique understanding of the present reality of God's unshakeable kingdom is context for them to live in the reality of their future resurrection through their personal incarnation of Jesus' Sermon on the Mount.

The extraordinary character of the believer, specified by Jesus in the Beatitudes (Mt. 5:3-12), provides the spiritual formation for obedience to Jesus' Sermon on the Mount:

- *The sacredness of human life is the single truth upon which everything Jesus says in the Sermon on the Mount is related—What does it mean to be human?* Our culture's vague notions of what it means to be human underlie absolutely every social issue in America today, e.g., religious, philosophical, political, racial, economical, educational and the rule of law. Therefore, the sacredness of human life is to be at the core of the ethical lives of Christians—*every* human life, from the moment

3. Ibid., 105.
4. Wright, *Jesus and the Victory of God*, 643.

of conception to the moment of death—possesses equal moral value simply because it is human.

- *The believer embraces marriage as a sacred covenant between one man and one woman, not because they desire to demean gay people but because the communal nature of the Divine Image—"God . . . created them; male and female. . ."—is uniquely revealed through the holy covenant of marriage.*

- *The believer's personal integrity is founded on their commitment to truth.* But what is truth? Christian truth is *not* founded on an impersonal, abstract cosmic principle but *truth is founded on God's revealed Word, both the Incarnation and the Scriptures; and faith, coupled with the Holy Spirit's regeneration and illumination.* Therefore, Biblical authority is at the heart of Christian conviction—*"Sanctify them by the truth; your word is truth"* (Jn. 14:6-7; 18:37; 17:17).

- *The reality of the sacredness of all human life, and the new humanity's desire to please God, compels them to unconditionally love their enemies.* Loving your enemy is not merely demonstrating good will towards others. To love your enemy "presupposes a social context of the faith-community encountering opposition, even persecution in society."[5]

Therefore, loving your enemy means, in relation to the Sermon on the Mount, believers never seek revenge—"an eye for an eye"—and the community of faith does not retaliate in the face of violence, but rather believers ". . . do good to those who hate [them], bless those who curse [them], pray for those who mistreat [them]" (Luke 6:27b-28).

To love your enemy was "tantamount to the rejection of the Zealot option"[6] in the first century context and it is tantamount to distinguishing Christian faith from the "Zealot option" in the twenty-first century context, radical Islam, or for that matter, the ideology of the radical far-left [or far-right] in the U.S.

- *Christian formation is basically founded on our faithfulness to three pillars adopted from Jewish piety: "When you give;" "When you pray," and "When you fast." The believer gives, prays and fasts with anonymity. Anonymity punctuates true righteousness in the kingdom of heaven.*

---

5. Chilton and McDonald, *Jesus and the Ethics of the Kingdom*, 102-103. In: Stassen & Gushee, *Kingdom Ethics*, 21-22.

6. Ibid., 22.

INSANITY!

The believer's faithfulness to these holy practices, when done in secret, that is, righteously, will be rewarded by God, our Father.

- *The heart of the disciple is not divided between two masters, but the eye of the disciple is "single," that is, the believer invests his or her "treasures" in God's kingdom of justice, mercy and humble service (cf. Lk. 4:4:18-19; Micah 6:8)—For where your treasure is, there your heart will be also."*

- *Lest they look past the plank in their own eye while pointing out the speck in another's eye, the disciple restrains themselves from too harshly judging another. The disciple is aware of their own criterion for faithful moral actions towards others and how flawlessly they themselves live up to the "measure" they may be tempted to use to judge another. (Perhaps the disciple's criterion is reflective of Wilberforce's practical application of the Golden Rule, cf., Ch. 14).*

- *No matter how dark the times in which we live, the believer trusts in the power of the Gospel and the finished work of Christ—The Cross is evidence that God cares about injustice and evil. Christian faith simply requires that* all *people acknowledge that because of their own sin—their willful unconformity to God's will for their life—they are incapable of* satisfying *God's ultimate justice and therefore, they need to turn to One who is both their Substitute and Justifier (cf., Rom. 3:21-26).*

The primary intent of this book is for believers to frame their lives in the Sermon on the Mount's ethic and live in its paradox reality—*Our daily lives are conditioned by both our connection to Jesus' historical resurrection and our future imperishable, immortal and incorruptible resurrection and that is the source of ultimate meaning for every ordinary day of our lives.* In relation to the Sermon on the Mount, this is the *normal* Christian life.

Through the power of God's Spirit, and the Sermon on the Mount taking narrative form in lives of believers, we do not merely survive in an increasingly secularizing, lawless, post-Christian culture, we thrive!

Our Nation's Renewed Acknowledgement Of God

By means of the Sermon on the Mount taking narrative form in a minority of believers' lives, the most pressing vision of this book is the renewal of our nation's acknowledgement of God and the consequent restoration of sanity and civility to our culture.

A Wise Builder

Os Guinness describes this vision of restored sanity and civility to our nation's public discourse: *". . . people of all faiths, whether religious or naturalistic—are equally free to enter and engage public life on the basis of their faiths, as a matter of 'free exercise' and as dictated by their own reason and conscience; but always within the double framework, first, of the Constitution, and second, of a freely and mutually agreed covenant or common vision for the common good, of what each person understands to be just and free for everyone else, and therefore of the duties involved in living with the deep differences of others."*[7]

The ideal of "the duties involved in living with the deep differences of others" is any believer in whose life the Sermon on the Mount is taking narrative form—*The Christian ethic, so eloquently delivered in the Sermon on the Mount, is the only ethic that acknowledges the full-moral equality of all humanity simply because they are human (re: Chapter 3, Murder and the Sacredness of Life: Mt. 5:21-26).*

What would a vision of the Sermon on the Mount taking narrative form in a minority of believers' lives ("the life of heaven") look like in a culture that was founded on its acknowledgement of God (et. al., the preamble of the Declaration of Independence) but no longer acknowledges Him and consequently, it is in the process of being turned over to itself?

In chapter 8, "Love Your Enemies, Mt. 5:43-48, my emphasis is on how a Western secularized city would see the church's good works through their obedience to Micah 6:8. What follows in this chapter is a vision of believers' personal integrity, *re:* my summary of the influence of the Sermon on the Mount in the believer's life above-mentioned.

Whereas the New Testament strongly testifies to the centrality of justice regarding the church's vocation (e.g., Matt. 25:31-46; Gal. 2:10; James 2:14-18), the Old Testament provides a vivid picture of the need for God's people to be God's *shālōm* in a culture in exile:

> This is what the Lord Almighty, the God of Israel, says to all those I carried into exile from Jerusalem to Babylon: "Build houses and settle down; plant gardens and eat what they produce. Marry and have sons and daughters; find wives for your sons and give your daughters in marriage, so that they too may have sons and daughters. Increase in number there; do not decrease. Also, seek the peace and prosperity of the city to which I have carried you into exile. Pray to the Lord for it, because if it prospers, you too will prosper," Jer. 29:1-7.

---

7. Guinness, *The Case for Civility,* 135.

INSANITY!

The Hebrew term translated "prosperity" (*shālēm*) is a derivative of the important Old Testament theological term translated "peace" (*shālōm*).[8] The root meaning of the verb *shālēm* expresses the true meaning of *shālōm*: "Completeness, wholeness, harmony, fulfillment are closer to the meaning."[9] Implicit in this understanding of the term *shālēm* is "unimpaired relationships with others and fulfillment in one's undertakings."[10] *God's covenant people were to incarnate the peace (shālōm) of God in Babylon.*

The term *shālēm* implies a surprising twist to the Jewish exile. The Babylonians, rather than the Jewish nation, were *really* in exile and God's covenant people were called to engage in meaningful relationships with these pagan people who were otherwise their natural enemies and make Babylon a good place to live.

Jesus, in the Sermon on the Mount, says to God's people—(Mt. 5):
[43] "You have heard that it was said, 'Love your neighbor and hate your enemy.' [44] But I tell you, love your enemies and pray for those who persecute you, [45] that you may be children of your Father in heaven."

Tim Keller tells a story about a Sri Lankan pastor named, Ajith Fernando. In 2004, anti-Christian rebels began assaulting believers and burning their churches; 150 Sri Lankan Christian Churches were burned.

Then, soon following the widespread persecution of Christians in Sri Lanka, a tsunami overcame the island and multitudes of people were killed; and a mass number of people were left homeless. The Sri Lankan Christians immediately went to the coastal areas and tirelessly gave themselves to an enormous relief effort.

Pastor Ajith said that one of his workers, a friend of his, helped a family that had been among those anti-Christian rebels who had burned so many churches down the year before. The man looked at Ajith's friend and said, "Last year we were assaulting you, and burning your churches, but we didn't know what you were really like."[11]

Because Christians in Sri Lanka were willing to love their enemies and seek the peace and prosperity of their pagan culture, the Sri Lankan people,

---

8. Harris, Gleason Jr. and Waltke, *Theological Wordbook of the Old Testament*, Vol. 2, entry 2401, 931.

9. Ibid.

10. Ibid.

11. Keller, "The Garden—City of God," Bible: The Whole Story—Redemption and Restoration—April 26, 2009, Revelation 22:1-9.

especially their enemies, were open to hearing the Gospel, the good news of the Savior of the world, Jesus Christ.

Only mature believers, possessed with the kind of Christian character described throughout this book and summarized above, are prepared to follow-through like Pastor Ajith and the believers in Sri Lanka. But these believers, described in the Sermon on the Mount and in this story, are not exceptional believers rather, this is the normal Christian life.

Therefore, if Israel was called by God to join the most decadent, depraved pagan nation on earth in its exile and to seek its "peace" and "prosperity," that is, to literally, love their enemies—and Sri Lankans loved God enough to love their enemies—ought not the American church willingly join our culture in its exile, especially our secularized cities, "like Portland or San Francisco or New York or L.A.," and be their "peace" and pray for their "prosperity," their *shālēm*?

"Whenever religion feels completely at home in the world, it is the salt which has lost its savor. If it sacrifices the strategy of renouncing the world, it has no strategy by which it may convict the world of sin."[12]—*But if the lives of a minority of unified believers were radically transformed by the Sermon on the Mount taking narrative form in them, the transformation of our nation would prove powerful enough to restore America to sanity and civility.*

Spiritual Formation

1. *Is the Sermon on the Mount taking narrative form in your life?*
2. *Spiritual formation (discipleship) requires obedience from God's people to the teachings of Jesus. What is your ministry, how are you a "wise builder" for others?*
3. *How can believers encourage and pray for one-another to help ensure that they thrive together in this post-Christian age?*
4. *What is the "mark" (that is, the fruit) of our thriving together in this post-Christian age?*

---

12. Reinhold, Niebuhr, *Does Civilization Need Religion?*, 166.

Appendix

America's Christian Heritage

"SHOULD OUR REPUBLIC EVER *forget this fundamental precept of governance,*" John Jay wrote about the importance of faith for virtue, *"men are certain to shed their responsibilities for licentiousness and this great experiment will surely be doomed."*[1]

Our nation's Christian heritage is evidenced not only in the words of our founders, but within the government buildings themselves. For example, the Ten Commandments hang over the head of the chief justice of the Supreme Court. In the House and Senate Chambers appear the words, "In God We Trust." On the walls of the Capitol dome appear the words, "The New Testament according to the Lord and Savior Jesus Christ." Engraved on the metal cap on the top of the Washington Monument are the words, "Praise be to God," and numerous Bible verses line the walls of the stairwell. And the Eighty-Third Congress set aside a room in the Capitol Building exclusively for the private prayer and meditation of members of Congress.

Our nation's most foundational documents, especially the Declaration of Independence, point to our Creator as our source of rights: "We hold these truths to be self-evident, that all men are created equal; that they are endowed by their Creator with certain unalienable rights; that among them are life, liberty, and the pursuit of happiness"—*Our unalienable rights are founded on divine absolutes and our special creation in God's image.*

Christians courageously stand for unalienable human rights, dignity and equality throughout the earth. Driven by her Christian roots, America is the greatest nation-building, world relief and benevolent nation in the history of the world.

1. Guinness, *A Free People's Suicide*, 117.

Appendix

Following the founding of the church itself, as an extension of Christ's resurrection, William Wilberforce led Great Britain in freeing slaves in all her colonies and England itself. Sierra Leone was created a slave-free state on the African continent through Wilberforce's original efforts to free slaves. Wilberforce was a great influence on many nations, to include Abraham Lincoln and the United States.

Roger Williams was heroic in his fighting for religious freedom for all; Elizabeth Fry reformed prisons, Dietrich Bonhoeffer resisted the evils of Nazism, Gary Haugen freed prisoners from modern sex trafficking and bonded slavery; and dared to believe that a better world was possible. And Martin Luther King Jr., a pastor from Atlanta, embodied kingdom virtues in the nonviolent African-American Civil Rights Movement in the 1960s.

And today, countless nations are served, in humanitarian, benevolent and compassionate ways, by Christian missionaries who although this world is unworthy of them, they will never be featured on any news outlet.

Further, Christian faith is the source for modern science and technology. Sir Francis Bacon, a devout believer in the Bible and Lord Chancellor of England, founded and established the "scientific method" by reference to the reality of the created order of the systems of the universe.

Following in the footsteps of Sir Francis Bacon, consider some of the great scientific discoveries and developments in science by men, who as Christians, interpreted their observations in accord with a Christian world view: Isaac Newton (dynamics); Johann Kepler (astronomy); Robert Boyle (chemistry); Lord Kelvin (thermodynamics); Louis Pasteur (bacteriology); Matthew Maury (electrodynamics); John Ray (biology); and Carolus Linnacus (taxonomy).

These scientific discoveries and developments were possible because of three basis axioms of science: "The first of the unprovable [self-evident] premises on which science has been based is the belief that the world is real and the human mind is capable of knowing its real nature; the second and best known postulate underlying the structure of scientific knowledge is that of cause and effect; and the third basic scientific premise is that nature is unified"[2] These three axioms are basically Christian in origin and nature, concludes Dr. Stanley D. Beck.[3]

---

2. Stanley D. Beck, "Natural Science and Creationist Theology," *Bio-Science* 32 (Oct. 1982), 739. Quoted in: Henry Morris, *The Biblical Basis for Modern Science*, 30-31.

3. Ibid.

The major divisions of science reflect the creation of the universe by the personal God of the Bible. The biblical commandment of God to man to take "dominion" over the earth (Genesis 1:28) is explained by Henry Morris: "There are only three specific acts of 'ex nihilo' creation recorded in Genesis, indicating three fundamentally different entities in God's universe. These acts are indicated by the use of the verb 'create' (Hebrew: *bara'*):

1. In the beginning God 'created' the heaven and the earth (Genesis 1:1).
2. God 'created' . . . every living creature that moves (Genesis 2:21).
3. God 'created' man in his own image (Genesis 1:27)."[4]

Genesis 1:1 refers to the creation of the world; and Genesis 2:21 relates to all living creatures except God's special creation in his own image as recorded in Genesis 1:27. These three major categories of God's creation provide a basis for the physical sciences, the life sciences, and the social sciences (inclusive of the humanities).[5]

The concept of the "dominion" mandate in Genesis (2:15;19-20) is the basis for many of the great scientific discoveries that benefit the Western world. Medical advancements, hospitals, the American Red Cross, and scores of national and international relief agencies and efforts are founded upon the Christian ethic and worldview.

And finally, the unified field of knowledge— the physical sciences, the life sciences, and the social sciences, to include the humanities (cf. Genesis 1:1,2:21,1:27), inherit in God's creation is the source for the great institutions of education in America. The IVY League Schools, owe their existence to the Judeo-Christian faith: every school, except one (Cornell), began as a training center, a Bible College/Seminary, for ministers.

The Puritans founded Harvard; and John Harvard, a Baptist Minister, donated his library to the upstart college in Massachusetts. Jonathan Edwards was the first president of The New Jersey State College (Princeton); Roger Williams founded Brown University; Brown's motto is: "In God we hope."

Columbia was a training center for Episcopal clergy. Columbia's founder, Samuel Johnson wrote (1754): "The chief thing that is aimed at in this college is to teach and engage the children to know God and Jesus

---

4. Henry Morris, *The Biblical Basis for Modern Science*, 42.
5. Ibid.

Appendix

Christ, and to love and serve him in all sobriety, godliness and righteousness of life with a perfect heart and a willing mind."

Penn's seal says: "Laws without morals are useless." The "Public Academy of Philadelphia" originated on property owned by George Whitefield. There, Benjamin Franklin oversaw the construction of a great preaching hall as the first building of what would become the University of Pennsylvania (the first graduating class was 7 people, 4 of which went into full time ministry).

Dartmouth's motto is: "A voice of one crying in the wilderness and one of the Yale founding presidents penned to his incoming students: "Above all, have an eye to the great end of all your studies which is to obtain the clearest conception of divine things and to lead you to a saving knowledge of God in His Son Jesus Christ."[6]

Every major cultural institution in the United States of America was founded on the Gospel. Civil religion is symbolic of the Gospel's influence in America.

Conclusion—Civil Religion

Themes of redemption are inextricably woven throughout the fabric of our nation's story. Civil religion is the cornerstone of our Republic. The Washington Monument memorializes the "father of our nation." Our nation's "father" is invisible; nowhere on the outside or inside of the monument is a picture of George Washington. The Monument's structure points towards the heavens and the profound *faith* Americans have in the religious heritage of our nation.

When one visits the Lincoln Memorial they first see the strong hands of our nation's savior who redeemed and restored the Republic and set the captives (the slaves) free. Inside the Monument, the walls are filled with Scriptures referring to redemption, restoration and resurrection; themes foundational to our nation's *hope*.

And was it accidental, or by design, that Martin Luther King Jr. delivered his, "I Have a Dream" speech in front of the Lincoln Memorial, as

---

6. Although some today attempt to trace the origin of universities back to Plato's Academy or the madrasa at Cairo's Al-Azhar Mosque, there is no doubt that the source behind the first universities in Bologna, the Sorbonne, Oxford and Cambridge was the rise of the cathedral schools in the late medieval world. Oxford's motto is founded on Psalm 27, *Dominus Illuminatio Mea*—"The Lord is my Light."

though he proceeds from the "Great Emancipator" and applies his finished work in the form of the Civil Rights Movement to those most in need: the oppressed, vulnerable and marginalized?

From redemptive themes in children's fairy tales such as Snow White and Cinderella, to Julia Roberts and the story of restoration in "Pretty Woman," to Denzel Washington and "Eli's Book," to the great monuments, the U.S. Capital Building, and the Supreme Court Building in Washington D.C., our nation's grand-narrative comprehends multiple layers of redemption stories that profoundly shape the US-American conscience.

Bibliography

Alexander, Brooks. "Occult Philosophy and Mystical Experience." *Spiritual Counterfeits Journal*. Winter, 1981-82.

Augustine. "The City of God." *Basic Writings of Saint Augustine*. Edited by, Whitney J. Oates. Vol. Two. Grand Rapids, MI.: Baker, 1948.

Bailey, D.S. *Homosexuality and the Western Christian Tradition*. London: Longmans, Green, 1955.

Barna Trends, 2017, What's New and What's Next at the Intersection of Faith and Culture (Grand Rapids, MI.: Baker Book House, 2016).

Batterson, Mark. *The Circle Maker, Praying Circles Around Your Biggest Dreams and Greatest Fears*. Grand Rapids, MI.: Zondervan, 2011.

Bauer, Walter, Arndt, William, Gingrich, Wilbur F., and Danker, Frederick W. *A Greek-English Lexicon of the New Testament and Other Early Christian Literature*. Chicago, IL.: The University of Chicago Press, 1958.

Beck, Stanley D. "Natural Science and Creationist Theology," *Bio-Science* 32. Oct. 1982.

Beckwith, Francis J. "Abortion and Public Policy: A Response to Some Arguments. Vol. 32. No. 4. December 1989.

———. *Politically Correct Death, Answering Arguments For Abortion Rights*. Grand Rapids, MI.: Baker, 1993.

———. "A Reply to the Moderate Evangelical Position on Abortion." *Journal of the Evangelical Theological Society*. Vol. 33. No. 4. December 1990.

Belcher, Jim. *Deep Church, A Third Way Beyond Emerging and Traditional*. Downers Grove, IL.: Inter-Varsity Press, 2009.

Belmonte, Kevin. *William Wilberforce, A Hero for Humanity*. Grand Rapids, MI: Zondervan, 2007.

Bonhoeffer, Dietrich. *The Cost of Discipleship*. New York, N.Y.: Simon & Schuster, 1959.

Boswell, J. *Christianity, Social Tolerance and Homosexuality*. Chicago: Chicago University, 1980.

Brown, F. S.R. Driver, and C.A. Briggs. *A Hebrew and English Lexicon*. Oxford: Clarendon, 1907.

Brown, Michael. https://en.wikipedia.org/wiki/Shooting_of_Michael_Brown, Downloaded: 07/18/2016.

Calvin, John. *Institutes of the Christian Religion*. Vols. 1-2. Edited by John T. McNeill. Philadelphia, PA: The Westminster Press, 1960.

Castro, Martin. "Civil Rights Commission: 'Religious Liberty,' 'Religious Freedom' Code Words for Intolerance, Homophobia, and 'Christian Supremacy. http://www.usccr.

Bibliography

gov/about/commissioners.php http://www.cnsnews.com/print/1261746 Page 1 of 2. Downloaded: 10/11/2016.

Chilton, Bruce and McDonald, J.I.H., *Jesus and the Ethics of the Kingdom* (Grand Rapids, MI.: Eerdmans, 1987).

Colson, Charles. *Colson Speaks, Key Messages from Today's Leading Defender of the Christian Faith.* Uhrichsville, OH.: Promise Press, An Imprint of Barbour Publishing, 2000.

Davies, W.D. and Dale Allison. *A Critical and Exegetical Commentary on the Gospel According to St. Matthew.* Vol. 1. Edinburgh: T & T Clark, 1998.

Department of Justice, Office of Public Affairs, U.S. Departments of Justice and Education Release Joint Guidance to Help Schools Ensure the Rights of Transgender Students. https://www.justice.gov/opa/pr/us-departments-justice-and-education-release-joint-guidancehelpschoolsensure-civil-rights. May 13, 2016. Downloaded: 06/20/2016. RrrrRightsgender Stude

DeYoung, James B. "The Meaning of 'Nature' in Romans 1 and Its Implications for Biblical Proscriptions of Homosexual Behavior." *Journal of the Evangelical Theological Society.* Vol. 31. No. 4. December 1988.

Dreher, Rod. "America: From Israel to Babylon," 10/29/2014, http://www.theamericanconservative.com/dreher/america-from-israel-to-babylon/. Downloaded: 01/04/2018.

Dubose, Samuel. https://en.wikipedia.org/wiki/Shooting_of_Samuel_DuBose, Down loaded: 07/18/2016.

Eck, Diana. "Honest to God," *God At 2000.* Marcus Borg & Ross Mackenzie, eds. Harrisburg, PA: Morehouse Publishing, 2000.

Elspeth. "The Age of Personal Peace and Affluence" Posted: April 16, 2013 https://traditionalchristianity.wordpress.com/2013/04/16/personal-peace-and-affluence/.

Fee, Gordon. *God's Empowering Presence.* Peabody, MA: Hendrickson, 1994.

———. *The First Epistle to the Corinthians, The New International Commentary On The New Testament.* Grand Rapids, MI: Wm. B. Eerdmans, 1987.

———. "The Kingdom of God." *Called and Empowered: Pentecostal Perspectives on Global Mission.* Murray Dempster, Byron D. Klause and Douglas Petersen, eds. Peabody, MA.: Hendrickson, 1992.

Fish, Stanley. *Doing What Comes Naturally: Change, Rhetoric and the Practice of Theory in Literary and Legal Studies.* Durham, N.C.: Duke University Press, 1989.

Foley, Dan. "Rachel Dolezal is Every Bit as Black as Caitlyn Jenner is Female." http://wfnt.com/rachel-dolezal-is-every-bit-as-black-as-caitlyn-jenner-is-female/. April 29, 2017. Downloaded: 04/28/2017.

Franke-Ruta, Garance. "Is Elizabeth Warren Native American or What?" https://www.theatlantic.com/politics/archive/2012/05/is-elizabeth-warren-native-american-or-what/257415/. May 20, 2012. Downloaded: 05/05/2017.

Frost, Michael & Alan Hirsch. *The Shaping of Things to Come, Innovation and Mission for the 21st—Century Church.* Peabody, MA.: Hendrickson Publishers, 2003.

Fukuyama, Francis. *Our Post-Human Future, Consequences of the Biotechnology Revolution.* New York, N.Y.: Picador, 2002.

Garner, Eric. https://en.wikipedia.org/wiki/Death of Eric_Garner, Downloaded: 07/18/2017.

Garza, Alicia, Cullors, Patrisse and Tometi, Opal, "A Herstory of the #BlackLivesMatter Movement," http://blacklivesmatter.com/herstory/, Downloaded: 08/09/2016.

BIBLIOGRAPHY

Gray, Freddie. https://en.wikipedia.org/wiki/Death_of_Freddie_Gray, Downloaded: 07/18/2016.

Grenz, Stanley J. "Jesus as the *Imago Dei:* Image-Of-God Christology and the Non-Linear Linearity of Theology." *Journal of the Evangelical Theological Society.* Vol. 47. No. 4. December 2004.

———. "Theological Foundations for Male-Female Relationships." *Journal of the Evangelical Theological Society.* Vol. 41. No. 4. December 1998.

Groothuis, Douglas. "Why Truth Matters Most: An Apologetic for Truth-Seeking in Postmodern Times." *Journal of the Evangelical Theological Society.* Vol. 47. No. 3. September 2004.

Guelich, Robert. *The Sermon on the Mount: A Foundation for Understanding.* Waco, Tex.: Word, 1982.

Guinness, Os. *A Free People's Suicide, Sustainable Freedom and the American Future.* Downers Grove, IL.: Inter-Varsity Press, 2012.

———. *Renaissance, The Power of the Gospel However Dark the Times.* Downers Grove, IL.: Inter-Varsity Press, 2014.

———. *The Case for Civility And Why Our Future Depends On It.* San Francisco, CA.: Harper-One, 2008.

Gundry, Robert H. *Matthew.* 2nd edition. Grand Rapids, MI.: William Eerdmans, 1994.

Gushee, David P. *The Sacredness of Human Life, Why An Ancient Biblical Vision Is Key to the World's Future.* Grand Rapids, MI.: William B. Eerdmans, 2013.

Haas, Guenther. "Perspectives on Homosexuality: A Review Article." *Journal of the Evangelical Theological Society.* Vol. 45. No. 3. September 2002.

Hancock, Christopher D. "The Shrimp Who Stopped Slavery." *Christian History.* 1997.

Harak, Simon G. S.J. *Virtuous Passions: The Formation of Christian Character.* New York, N.Y.: Paulist Press, 1993

Harris, R. Laird, Gleason L. Archer, Jr., Bruce K. Waltke. *Theological Wordbook of the Old Testament,* Vol. I. Chicago, IL.: Moody Press, 1980.

———. *Theological Wordbook of the Old Testament,* Vol. II. Chicago, IL.: Moody Press, 1980.

Harrison, R.K. General Editor. *Encyclopedia of Biblical and Christian Ethics.* Nashville. TN. Thomas Nelson, 1987.

Hess, Monica. "How The Bathroom Became a Political Battleground for Civil Rights." *The Washington Post,* https://www.washingtonpost.com/lifestyle/style/why-america-cant-stop-fighting-over-the-politics-of-public-restrooms/2016/04/01/16af2f94-f6b6-11e5-a3ce-f06b5ba21f33_story.html. Page 3 of 10. Downloaded: 06/20/2016.

Hick, John. *A Christian Theology of Religions.* Louisville, KY: Westminster John Knox Press, 1995.

———. *Truth and Dialogue.* London: Sheldon, 1974.

Hill, Clifford. *The Wilberforce Connection.* Oxford, UK, Monarch, 2004.

Hitler, Adolf. *Mein Kampf,* tr. Ralph Manaheim, Houghton Miffin, n.d.

Howse, Ernest Marshall. *Saints in Politics: The Clapham Sect and the Growth of Freedom.* George Allen and Unwin, 1952.

Hurkman, *Venture Expeditions,* Sermon delivered at: Cedar Valley Assembly of God, January 13, 2013. Please see: "Venture: Events, Expeditions, Adventures," http://www.ventureexpeditions.org.

Imago Dei Community: http://www.imagodeicommunity.com, 11/15/2007.

Bibliography

Jersild, Paul T. and Dale A. Johnson. Editors. *Moral Issues and Christian Response.* Third Edition. New York, N.Y.: CBS College, 1983.

Kaiser Jr., Walter. *Toward Old Testament Ethics.* Grand Rapids, MI.: Zondervan, 1983.

———. *What Does The Lord Require?* Grand Rapids, MI.: Baker Academic, 2009.

Keener, Craig. *Matthew,* Editors: Grant R. Osborne, D. Stuart Briscoe and Haddon Robinson. Downers Grove, IL.: Inter-Varsity Press, 1997.

Keller, Tim. "There Can't Be Just *One* True Religion." *The Reason for God, Belief in an Age of Skepticism.* New York, NY: Dutton, 2008.

Kelly, J.N.D. *Early Christian Creeds.* London: Longman's, 1950.

Kierkegaard, Soren. *The Point of View.* Translated by W. Lowie. London: Oxford University Press,1939.

Kilner, John F. *Dignity and Destiny, Humanity in the Image of God.* Grand Rapids, MI: William B. Eerdmans, 2015.

King, Luther Jr., 1965, "The American Dream." Sermon July 4, Ebenezer Baptist Church, Atlanta, GA., http://www.sweetspeeches.com/s/309-martin-luther-king-jr-the-american-dream#.

Kinnaman, David. *Barna Trends, 2017, What's New and What's Next at the Intersection of Faith and Culture.* Grand Rapids, MI.: Baker Book House, 2016.

Kirby,Alan. "Successor States To An Empire In Free Fall." https://www.timeshighereducation.com/features/successor-states-to-an-empire-in-free-fall/411731.article. May 27, 2010. Downloaded: 05/03/2016.

Kittel, Gerhard, ed. *Theological Dictionary of the New Testament.* Vol. I. Grand Rapids, MI.: Eerdmans, 1964.

———. *Theological Dictionary of the New Testament.* Vol. II. Grand Rapids, MI.: Eerdmans, 1964.

———. *Theological Dictionary of the New Testament.* Vol. III. Grand Rapids, MI.: Eerdmans, 1965.

———. *Theological Dictionary of the New Testament.* Vol. IV. Grand Rapids, MI.: Eerdmans, 1967.

Kittel, Gerhard & Gerhard Friedrich, eds. *Theological Dictionary of the New Testament.* V. Grand Rapids, MI.: Eerdmans, 1967.

———. *Theological Dictionary of the New Testament.* Edited by: Gerhard Kittel & Gerhard Friedrich. VI. Grand Rapids, MI.: Eerdmans, 1968.

———. *Theological Dictionary of the New Testament.* VII. Grand Rapids, MI.: Eerdmans, 1971.

———. *Theological Dictionary of the New Testament.* VIII. Grand Rapids, MI.: Eerdmans, 1972.

———. *Theological Dictionary of the New Testament.* IX. Grand Rapids, MI.: Eerdmans, 1974.

Kohlhepp, Jacob. "California Students Now Given Six 'Gender Identity' Choices On College Admissions Applications." http://www.thecollegefix.com/post/23519/. 11/23/2016. Downloaded: 11/25/2016.

Kristof, Nicholas. "Am I a Christian, Pastor Timothy Keller?" *New York Times.* Dec. 23, 2016. http://www.nytimes.com/2016/12/23/opinion/sunday/pastor-am-i-a-christian.html?_r=1. Downloaded: 04/02/2017.

Kuehne, Dale. *Sex and the I-World: Rethinking Relationship in an Age of Individualism.* Grand Rapids: Baker Academic, 2009.

BIBLIOGRAPHY

Louw, Johannes P. & Eugene A. Nida. *Greek-English Lexicon of the New Testament*, Vol. 1. New York: United Bible Societies, 1989, Second Ed.

Lukianoff, Greg and Jonathan Haidt. *The Atlantic*. https://www.theatlantic.com/magazine/archive/2015/09/the-coddling-of-the-american-mind/399356. September 2015. Downloaded: 07/21/2016.

Luther, Martin. *The Smalcald Articles*, Part 1, Statement 1.

———. *The Sermon on the Mount*. 1521: Translated by Jaroslav Pelikan. Vol. 21 of *Luther's Works*. Concordia, 1956.

Luther King Jr., Martin. *Strength to Love*. Minneapolis, MN.: Fortress, 1981.

———. "The American Dream." Sermon July 4, Ebenezer Baptist Church, Atlanta, GA. http://www.sweetspeeches.com/s/309-martin-luther-king-jr-the-american-dream#.

Lyotard, Jean-Francois. *The Postmodern Condition: A Report on Knowledge*. "Theory and History of Literature," Volume 10. Minneapolis, MN.: University of Minnesota Press, 1984.

McDonald, Laquan, http://www.nbcchicago.com/news/local/Police-Release-Disturbing-Video-of-Officer-Fatally-Shooting-Chicago-Teen-352231921.html, Downloaded: 08/09/2016.

"Martin Luther King Jr., And the Global Freedom Struggle,Civil Rights Acts, 1964," http://kingencyclopedia.stanford.edu/encyclopedia/encyclopedia/enc_civil_rights_act_of_1964/. Downloaded: 03/11/2017.

McRoberts, Kerry D. *New Age or Old Lie?* Peabody, MA.: 1989.

———. "The Holy Trinity." *Systematic Theology, Pentecostal Perspectives*, Edited by Stanley Horton. Springfield, MO.: Logion Press, 1994.

———. "The 'Sign of Jonah': Beyond Reasonable Doubt?" *A Letter From Christ, Apologetics in Cultural Transition*. New York, N.Y.: University Press, 2012.

———. "William Wilberforce and 'Vital Christianity.'" *Recovering The Church's Vocation: Following Jesus To Burning Man*. Lanham, MD.: Hamilton, 2011.

Meyers, David G. *Psychology*, 9th ed. New York: Worth Publishers, 2009.

Montgomery, John W. *Human Rights & Human Dignity*. Grand Rapids, MI.: Zondervan, 1986.

Moreland, J.P. "Truth, Contemporary Philosophy, and the Postmodern Turn." *Journal of the Evangelical Theological Society*. Vol. 48. No. 1. March 2005.

Morris, Henry. *The Biblical Basis for Science*. Grand Rapids, MI.: Baker, 1984.

Nicholson, R.A., Translator. *Rami: Poet and Mystic*. London: Unwin's Mandala Books, 1978.

Niebuhr, Reinhold. *Does Civilization Need Religion? A Study in the Social Resources and Limitations of Religion in Modern Life*. New York, NY.: MacMillan, 1927.

Osborne, Grant R. Series Editor. *Matthew*. Downers Grove, IL.: Inter-Varsity Press, 1997.

Packer, J.I. *Concise Theology, A Guide To Historic Christian Beliefs*. Wheaton, IL.: Tyndale House Publishers, 1993.

Pastor, Paul J. "John Mark Comer, The Westside: Bridgetown." *Outreach Magazine.com*. *The 2016 Outreach 100*.

———. "Rick McKinley, The Eastside: Imago Dei." *Outreach,100 Fastest Growing Churches in America*. 36.

Perkins, John. *Let Justice Roll Down*. New York, N.Y.: Regal, 1977.

———. Editor. *Restoring At Risk Communities*. Grand Rapids, MI.: Baker, 1995.

Reeves, Carol. "God at 2000." *Gazette-Times*, Corvallis, Oregon, February 12, 2000.

BIBLIOGRAPHY

Response. "A Conversation with N.T. Wright." Summer 2002, Vol. 28, Number 2. http://www.spu.edu/depts/uc/response/summer2k5/features/conversation.asp. Seattle Pacific University. Downloaded: 08/15/2005.

Robertson, Archibald Thomas. "The Epistles of Paul." *Word Pictures in the New Testament*, Volume VI. Grand Rapids, MI.: Baker Book House, 1931.

Ross, Chuck. "Black Lives Protesters Chant: 'Pigs In A Blanket Fry 'Em Like Bacon,'" http://dailycaller.com/2015/08/29/black-lives-matter-protesters-chant-pigs-in-a-blanket-fry-em-like-bacon-video/, Downloaded: 08/09/2016.

Schaeffer, Francis. "Christian Faith and Human Rights," 5. Cf. S.R. Mohan Das, "Discrimination in India," *Case Studies on Human Rights and Fundamental Freedoms*, ed. Veenhoven.

———. "How Should We Then Live – 09. The Age of Personal Peace and Affluence." https://vimeo.com/20178941. Downloaded: 05/18/2017.

———. "The Church at the End of the Twentieth Century." *The Complete Works of Francis A. Schaeffer, A Christian View of The Church*, Vol. 4. Westchester, IL.: Crossway Books, 1982.

Scroggs, R. *The New Testament and Homosexuality*. Philadelphia: Fortress, 1983.

Smith, James K.A. *Who's Afraid of Postmodernism?* Grand Rapids, MI.: Baker Academic, 2006.

Smith, Wesley J. "The Human Exceptionalism—July 2012," July 31, 2012. https://www.discovery.org/human/. Downloaded: 08-10-2015.

Sommerville, C. John. *The Decline of the Secular University*. New York, N.Y.: Oxford University Press, 2006.

Spinkle, Joe M. "Sexuality, Sexual Ethics," *Dictionary of the Old Testament: Pentateuch*, Editors, T. Desmond Alexander and David W. Baker. Downers Grove, IL: Inter-Varsity Press, 2003.

Stassen, Glen H. & David P. Gushee. *Following Jesus in Contemporary Context, Kingdom Ethics*. Downers Grove, IL.: Inter-Varsity, 2003.

Stott, John. Dale & Sandy Larsen. *A Deeper Look at the Sermon on the Mount, Living Out The Way of Jesus*. Downers Grove, IL.: Inter-Varsity Press, 2013.

———. *The Message of the Sermon on the Mount*. Downers Grove, IL.: Inter-Varsity Press, 1978.

Swindoll, Charles. *A Man of Passion & Destiny, David*. Nashville, TN.: Thomas Nelson, 1997.

Tallman, Matt & Cheryl. Open Arms International. www.OpenArmsInternational.com.

Tasker, R.V.G. *The Gospel According to St. Matthew*. Downers Grove, IL.: Inter-Varsity Press, 1961.

Taylor, R.O.P. *The Athanasian Creed in the Twentieth Century*. Edinburgh: T.&T. Clark, 1911.

Temple, Archbishop William. *Towards an Evangelical Public Policy*.

The Catholic World Report. "Essential Excerpts from 'Obergefell v. Hodges': Majority Opinion." http://www.catholicworldreport.com/2015/07/15/essential-excerpts-from-obergefell-v-hodges-majority-opinion/ July 15, 2015 CWR Staff, 2 of 4. Downloaded: 03/15/2016.

Vaughan, David J. *Statesman and Saint: The Principled Politics of William Wilberforce*. Nashville, TN.: Highland, 2002.

Voltaire [Francois Marie Arouet]. 1880. *Le Sottisier*. Paris: Librairie des bibliophiles.

Bibliography

Waltke, Bruce. "Reflections From The Old Testament On Abortion." Evangelical Theological Society, http://www.etsjets.org/files/JETS-PDFs/19/19-1/19-1-pp003-014_JETS.pdf, December 29, 1975.

Warfield, Benjamin B. *Studies in Tertullian and Augustine*. Westport, CT.: Greenwood Press, 1970.

Watson, Paul Joseph. "SICK: 'Black Lives Matter' Support Celebrate Murder of Dallas Cops." http://www.infowars.com/sick-black-lives-matter-supporters-celebrate-murder-of-dallas-cops/. July 8, 2016, Downloaded: 08/09/2016.

Wilberforce, William. *A Practical View of Christianity*. Peabody, MA: Hendrickson, 1996.

Willard, Dallas. *Divine Conspiracy, Rediscovering our Hidden Life in God*. San Francisco, CA: Harper, 1997.

Wilson, Douglas. "Southern Baptist Lava Lamps." Wednesday, June 15, 2016, https://www.facebook.com/sharer.php?u=https%3A%2F%2Fdougwils.com%2Fs7-engaging-the-culture%2Fsouthern-baptist-lava-lamps.html&t=Southern%20Baptist%20Lava%20 Lamps downloaded: 07/17/2017.

Witherington III, Ben. *Paul's Letter to the Romans, A Socio-Rhetorical Commentary* Grand Rapids, MI: Wm. B. Eerdmans, 2004.

What is Cultural Marxism? European-Unity, 565, May 14, 2016, https://www.youtube.com/watch?v=G8pPbrbJJQs, downloaded: 09/22/2017.

Wikimedia. Martin Luther King Jr. And the Global Freedom Struggle,Civil Rights Acts, 1964," http://kingencyclopedia.stanford.edu/encyclopedia/encyclopedia/enc_civil_ rights_act_of_1964/Downloaded: 03/11/2017.

Wikipedia, https://en.wikipedia.org/wiki/Black_Lives_Matter, Downloaded: 08/09/2016.

Wolff, Robert Paul II, Barrington Moore Jr., Herbert Marcuse. *A Critique of Pure Tolerance*. Boston, MA.: Beacon Press, 1965.

http://www.marcuse.org/herbert/pubs/60spubs/1965MarcuseRepressiveToleranceEng19 69edOcr.pdf, Downloaded: 09/22/2017.

Wright, N.T. *After You Believe, Why Christian Character Matters*. New York, N.Y.: Harper-One, 2010.

———. *Evil and the Justice of God*. Downers Grove, IL.: Inter-Varsity Press, 2006.

———. *Jesus and the Victory of God*. Minneapolis, MN., Fortress 1996.

———. *The Resurrection of the Son of God*. Minneapolis, MN.: Fortress, 2003.

Yiannopoulos, Milo. "Riots Break Out at UC Berkeley Amid Protests of Breitbart Editor's Speech." https://www.rt.com/usa/376001-milo-yiannopoulos-berkeley-riot-protest/. 2 Feb. 2017. Downloaded: 02/06/2017.

Zacharias, Ravi. *Jesus Among Other Gods*. Nashville, TN: Word Publishing, 2000.

Zimmerman, Brian. Street-Lite Christian Fellowship. http://www.streetlite.com/who-we-are/our-vision/. Downloaded: 06/15/2017.

www.ingramcontent.com/pod-product-compliance
Lightning Source LLC
Chambersburg PA
CBHW072143160426
43197CB00012B/2223